BOXER

TERRY ALBERT

Boxer

Editor: Stephanie Fornino
Indexer: Elizabeth Walker
Designer: Patricia Escabi
Series Designer: Mary Ann Kahn

TFH Publications®
President/CEO: Glen S. Axelrod
Executive Vice President: Mark E. Johnson
Publisher: Christopher T. Reggio
Production Manager: Kathy Bontz

TFH Publications, Inc.®
One TFH Plaza
Third and Union Avenues
Neptune City, NJ 07753

Discovery Communications, Inc. Book Development Team: Marjorie Kaplan, President and General Manager, Animal Planet Media / Kelly Day, EVP and General Manager, Discovery Commerce / Elizabeth Bakacs, Vice President, Licensing and Creative / JP Stoops, Director, Licensing / Bridget Stoyko, Associate Art Director

Printed and bound in China

12 13 14 15 16 17 1 3 5 7 9 8 6 4 2

Library of Congress Cataloging-in-Publication Data
Albert, Terry, 1951-
  Boxer / Terry Albert.
    p. cm.
  Includes bibliographical references and index.
  ISBN 978-0-7938-3723-6 (alk. paper)
  1. Boxer (Dog breed) I. Title.
  SF429.B75A43 2011
  636.73--dc22
                                    2011012368

This book has been published with the intent to provide accurate and authoritative information in regard to the subject matter within. While every reasonable precaution has been taken in preparation of this book, the author and publisher expressly disclaim responsibility for any errors, omissions, or adverse effects arising from the use or application of the information contained herein. The techniques and suggestions are used at the reader's discretion and are not to be considered a substitute for veterinary care. If you suspect a medical problem consult your veterinarian.

Note: In the interest of concise writing, "he" is used when referring to puppies and dogs unless the text is specifically referring to females or males. "She" is used when referring to people. However, the information contained herein is equally applicable to both sexes.

The Leader In Responsible Animal Care for Over 50 Years!®
www.tfh.com

CONTENTS

ORIGINS OF
YOUR BOXER

The Boxer is a versatile breed with a colorful history. He's a bold guard dog one minute and a wiggling, kissy-faced friend the next. But more than anything else, he is devoted to those he loves. An intelligent breed with an outstanding work ethic, Boxers have served the military, police force, and people with disabilities with equal ability. In his distant past he filled roles in the circus and bull-baiting rings, performing tricks or battling opponents with enthusiasm. To really understand the 21st-century Boxer, we need to trace the evolution of man and dog through the centuries and look at the forces that shaped our breed.

THE DEVELOPMENT OF THE DOG

Most historians agree that dogs originated in Central Asia near Tibet, descending from wolves that wandered the earth during the Pleistocene era between 10,000 and 60,000 years ago. At this time, humans were nomadic hunter-gatherers. They migrated, searching for food, and their leftover bones and other waste attracted the scavenging wolves to their camps. The tribes benefited from their new canine companions who, with their keen sense of smell and hearing, alerted the nomads to approaching predators and game they then killed for food.

Although some of the wolves were probably eaten, others became acclimated to people. Those that were the least threatening had litters that were brought into the camps and raised. In time, civilization evolved from hunting and gathering

Many historians believe that dogs descended from wolves that wandered the earth during the Pleistocene era.

Throughout history, Boxers have been praised for their intelligence, good disposition, and trainability.

to more permanent settlements and agricultural communities. Humans began selectively breeding those wolves that were least aggressive and had other desirable characteristics. The resulting canines were used as draft animals, livestock guardians, and hunting companions—in other words: domesticated.

Historians believe that some of the Tibetan dogs, like many of the other animals of that era, developed into very large animals. All of the world's mastiff breeds (including Boxers) have descended from this big Tibetan stock. As migration began around the world, traders followed an ancient route through Lhasa, Katmandu, and India and over water into Bahrain and Mesopotamia (present-day Iraq). The dogs who accompanied them were traded for supplies along the way.

The Assyrian kingdom in northern Mesopotamia of 2300 to 600 BC used these heavy dogs for war, giving them the name "Molossers" after the city of Molossus in ancient Greece. The Molossian dogs had a wide short muzzle and protruding lower jaw. This facial structure is still evident in Boxers and other breeds today. Traders and migrating Assyrians took Molosser dogs with them to Egypt and what later became Turkey and Rome, and north into the European continent.

THE BOXER IN GERMANY

By the Middle Ages, one type of Molosser, called a Bullenbeisser (bull-baiter) or Barenbeisser (bear-baiter), was used as a hunting dog in Germany. The

Bullenbeisser's powerful jaws could hang on to large prey like bear, deer, boar, or bison. He didn't let go until the animal was exhausted and the hunter arrived to complete the kill. Besides hunting, the Bullenbeisser was a popular contender in the new sports of bull-baiting and dogfighting.

Some of the dogs were gradually bred smaller through natural selection. Now split between a large and small Bullenbeisser, the shorter dog was a more courageous and efficient fighter. Owners cropped the dogs' ears and docked their tails so that they wouldn't be torn off in combat. Through the 17th to 19th centuries, the Bullenbeisser continued to be a popular hunting, fighting, and guard dog for the nobility. Butchers and cattle dealers also used them as guard dogs and to round up animals around the slaughterhouse.

We don't know for sure how the name "Boxer" came about, but by 1850 the name referred to the small Bullenbeisser and Bulldog-type dogs of Germany. "Der Boxer" translates to "the pugilist," and since they were fighting dogs, the name was appropriate. Others claim that the name came about because Boxers "box" with their front feet, although they also employ head butts and body-slamming moves.

Throughout this fierce history, Boxers were praised for their intelligence, good disposition, and trainability. By the late 1800s they were often seen in circus acts and theater. Meanwhile, their popularity as family pets grew as people recognized their devotion to their owners and almost human-like ability to communicate.

WHITE BOXERS

White Boxers have existed since the beginning of the breed. In the 19th century, English Bulldogs were imported into Germany and frequently crossed with Boxers. Bulldogs of that era didn't look like the Bulldogs of today. They had heavy bodies and long legs and were built more like small Mastiffs. After Bulldogs were introduced, more white Boxers began to appear. Later Boxer breeders worked hard to breed out Bulldog traits, but the white coloring remained and is still common today.

English Bulldogs appear in the pedigrees of some of the first registered Boxers from the 1890s: Dr. Toenniessen's Tom and Trutzel. Several of the foundation dogs of the Boxer breed—like Meta von der Passage and Flock St. Salvador—were white or white with fawn or brindle patches.

White wasn't considered a good color for a guard dog, the Boxer's primary function, because white dogs were too easy to see in the dark. The German Boxer Club declared white a disqualification in 1925.

White Boxers have existed since the beginning of the breed.

THE GERMAN BOXER CLUB

The first Boxer breed club was established in Munich, Germany, in 1896. Several more clubs soon followed, and in 1905 they merged to form the German Boxer Club. The club then established an official breed standard, which is a physical description of the ideal Boxer. The heavy-boned mastiff-like characteristics gradually evolved into an elegant, lighter-boned profile. Today's Boxer looks much as it has since the early 20th century.

THE FIRST OFFICIAL BOXERS

Breeding started slowly in Germany from a small gene pool of just a few closely related Boxers. Today their names are found in the pedigrees of more than 95 percent of all Boxers throughout the world. Almost from the beginning, Germans prized the working ability of their dogs. The early Boxers were smart and trainable, and breeders strived to retain these talents. In order to earn the Sieger (champion) title, dogs were required to pass a test demonstrating those qualities.

BOXERS IN WORLD WAR I

As Germany entered the first World War, Boxer owners readied their dogs for army service. They turned their efforts from showing to training their dogs in Schutzhund, a discipline that combines obedience, tracking, and protection work. Boxers were called to the front in 1914 to serve as sentries and messenger dogs. Siegers were the first dogs chosen because they already had training certificates. Many Siegers died on the battlefields in both World Wars.

One such champion, Rolf von Vogelsberg, survived WWI and came back to continue his show career. Owned by Philip and Friederun Stockmann, Rolf was one of the most notable Boxers of his time, siring champions and earning two additional Sieger titles following the war. After the war, Frau Stockmann began to show and breed Rolf's descendants. Their kennel, von Dom, became a major force in the development of Boxers, producing many of the top Boxers in the world during the first half of the 20th century. While her husband served in both wars, Frau Stockmann trained her Boxers for military work.

Partly because of their accomplishments during WWI, the Boxer's reputation for intelligence and trainability spread. They were accepted as police dogs in 1925. In 1926 Boxers also began serving as the first Seeing Eye Dogs for the blind.

BOXERS IN WORLD WAR II

After the Nazi takeover in 1933, the Organization for German Dogs regulated breeding and ownership. The group issued a new regulation stating that in order to be bred, a dog had to hold a Schutzhund degree. Once again, dogs were going to be used for military purposes. When the war began, all dogs had to be registered, and only those who passed inspection by a breed warden were awarded ration cards for food. Some dogs were sent out of the country or just killed by their owners. Luckily, many dogs went to work. Thousands of Boxers were used as sentries, messengers, pack dogs, mine detectors, and rescue dogs.

THE BOXER IN THE UNITED STATES

The first record of a Boxer in the United States is in 1898, when two were shown at the Westminster Kennel Club dog show. The first Boxer registered in the US was Arnulf Grandenz, in 1904, an American dog born from a German import. The breed was slow getting established in the US. The first Boxer to achieve a championship in the United States was Sieger Dampf von Dom in 1915, a brindle dog born in 1912 and exported to the US by the Stockmanns.

Between 1919 and 1924, no Boxers were registered in the US, and registrations stayed low throughout the 1920s.

Boxers were called to the front in World War I to serve as sentries and messenger dogs.

THE FOUR HORSEMEN OF BOXERDOM

But interest picked up in the 1930s, when four outstanding Boxers were imported from Germany. These "four horsemen of Boxerdom" became the foundation of the American Boxer.

Sigurd von Dom was first to arrive in 1934, at age five. At that time, the Third Reich was gaining power in Germany. Money for supplies to feed and care for dogs was tight, and Frau Stockmann did the only thing she could, given the circumstances. When a wealthy American offered to buy Sigurd, she felt she had to accept the offer. When Sigurd reached America he continued his show career and quickly became a popular Boxer stud dog.

Sigurd was grandsire to three great German Boxers who later followed him to the United States: Dorian von Marienhof (arrived 1936), Lustig von Dom (1937), and Utz von Dom (1939). Dorian won the Working Group at Westminster in 1937 and sired 40 champions in the US. Lustig became an

The American Boxer Club (ABC) was formed in February 1935.

American champion within a week of his first show and sired 41 champions. Utz won the Working Group at Westminster in 1940 and sired 37 champions.

As you see, the Stockmanns' (von Dom) dogs influenced the breed in America as well as Germany. But in 1939, war broke out in Europe and importation came to a halt.

BREED RECOGNITION

The American Boxer Club (ABC) was formed in February 1935. In May of that same year, the American Kennel Club (AKC) granted official status to the club. In September 1935 the AKC moved the Boxer from the Non-Sporting Group to the Working Group.

In 1938 Philip Stockmann visited the United States to judge 102 Boxers entered at the Westminster show. A group of American Boxer Club members recruited him to translate the German standard and assist them in rewriting the American standard. Because so many Boxers were imported, it made sense that the two standards should complement each other. The revised standard went into effect in May 1938.

BOXERS IN WWII SERVE THE ALLIED FORCES

The United States hadn't prepared dogs for war service and scrambled to catch up once WWII began. Many Boxers joined the thousands of German Shepherd Dogs, Doberman Pinschers, and Belgian Malinois who served in all branches of the armed forces. Owners proudly donated their family pets for war work. Illustrations and photos of Boxers in action were depicted on patriotic

As the years have passed, the Boxer has steadily become more popular.

posters. One photo from the US Army Corps of Engineers features a photo of a Boxer parachuting behind enemy lines in Europe.

In November 1946, Punch and Judy, a Boxer dog and bitch, received the British Dickin Medal, considered the canine equivalent of the Victoria Cross. Instituted by Mrs. Maria Dickin, the award was presented to any animal displaying conspicuous gallantry and devotion to duty associated with the armed forces during WWII and its aftermath. Their award reads: "These dogs saved the lives of two British officers in Israel by attacking an armed terrorist who was stealing upon them unawares and thus warning the officers of their danger. Punch sustained 4 bullet wounds and Judy a long graze down her back."

THE GOLDEN AGE OF BOXERS

In 1934 only 64 Boxers were registered, but by 1946 the breed was ranked number five in AKC registrations. In 1947 Ch. Warlord of Mazelaine (sired by Utz von Dom) became the first Boxer to win Best in Show at Westminster. Ten thousand Boxers were registered that year; the Golden Age of Boxers was in full swing. Boxers continued to win, taking Westminster in 1949 and 1951. The breed was often the largest entry in shows nationwide from 1946 to 1956.

CH. BANG AWAY OF SIRRAH CREST

Frau Stockmann visited the United States in 1949, and while judging at a match in Southern California, a four-month-old Boxer caught her eye. She recognized him as a descendant of her beloved Lustig, another dog she had been forced to sell before the war. She referred to the pup as "Little Lustig" and gave him first prize. That dog, Bang Away of Sirrah Crest, went on to become the most famous Boxer in American history, winning Westminster in 1951. He appeared on the covers of many national magazines, including *Vanity Fair*, *Life*, *Esquire*, *Sports Illustrated*, and *Time*. Bang Away sired 81 champions and won 121 Best in Show awards. Even today, Boxer breeders get misty-eyed when they tell tales of his charisma in the ring. Many feel that he single-handedly changed the breed forever with his attitude and beauty.

AFTER BANG AWAY

The January 1950 AKC *Gazette* reported a vaudeville act of 14 basketball-playing Boxers. When the owner, Rudy Docky, originally of Austria, lived in Europe, he had a soccer-playing Boxer act. But soccer wasn't popular in the United States, so he

Gradually, more Boxers with natural ears are appearing in the US show ring and winning ribbons.

switched his act to basketball. At the end of each performance, he pulled a bunch of balloons down from the ceiling. The Boxers pounced and played, bursting them as the curtain came down. He swore that Boxers were the smartest breed and would own nothing else.

By 1950 Boxers were ranked number two in popularity of AKC breeds, with more than 21,000 registered. Their popularity as a family pet did not drop off until the 1970s, when Boxers dropped out of the top 20 for several years. By 1990 the breed's popularity steadily moved back up in the ranks, remaining in the top ten for most of the first decade in the 21st century.

WHITE BOXERS COME OF AGE

White Boxers are once again an officially recognized part of the Boxer family in the US. Until 2005, white Boxers could not be registered at all or even sold. The American Boxer Club (ABC) Code of Ethics required that they be given away to pet homes. The 2005 revision states that white puppies are now eligible for AKC Limited Registration. They are recognized as purebred Boxers, but any puppies produced cannot be registered.

CROPPING AND DOCKING

Germany banned ear cropping in 1990 and tail docking in 1998. Other European countries, including Great Britain, have instituted similar bans. In the United States both practices are still legal, and most of the dogs you see in the show ring have cropped ears and docked tails.

When the revised standard of 2005 was implemented, dogs with natural ears became eligible to compete in conformation. Gradually, more are appearing in the show ring and winning ribbons. In 2011 a Grand Champion Boxer with natural ears was shown at Westminster for the first time. Natural ears have also become more popular with pet owners.

But some traditions die hard; the national club doesn't allow undocked tails, and you won't see them very often, if at all, in the US.

BREED CLUBS

The American Boxer Club (www.americanboxerclub.org) is the parent club of the breed in the United States and is now more than 75 years old. Fifty-four regional clubs support the ABC. Members show their dogs in conformation and performance events. The ABC maintains a code of ethics that guides breeders in responsible breeding practices. It encourages breeding for sound temperament and endorses health testing to identify genetically inherited diseases in

The American Boxer Club (ABC) maintains a code of ethics that guides breeders in responsible breeding practices.

potential breeding dogs. The club also sets standards for humane dog care and sportsmanlike conduct.

An offshoot of the ABC is the Boxer Charitable Health Foundation, which funds research into Boxer health issues.

The United States Boxer Association (www.usboxer.org) is a smaller club and is dedicated to preserving the Boxer's working heritage. If you are interested in Schutzhund training, this is the place to start. The club sponsors events throughout the United States. Called the USA-BOX for short, the club is a member of the American Working Dog Federation (AWDF) (www.awdf.net) and ATIBOX.

ATIBOX (www.atibox-online.net) is an international association of Boxer clubs. Shows are usually held in European countries and feature sparring in the conformation ring. The dogs, held by a 7- to 8-foot (2- to 2.5-m) line, are allowed to face off against each other in a controlled confrontation (not fighting). They should be alert and show off so that the judge can see how they carry themselves when not being formally posed by a handler. Sparring is common in the United States in AKC terrier breed classes but never with Boxers. In recent years ATIBOX has added performance events such as obedience and Schutzhund. ATIBOX is a member of the Fédération Cynologique Internationale (FCI) (www.fci.be). Established in 1911, the FCI maintains member clubs all over the world, including the United States, and subscribes to different breed standards than the AKC does.

CHARACTERISTICS
OF YOUR BOXER

The Boxer is a dignified, sturdy dog developed to hunt game, guard the home, and serve as a family companion. He does all three with grace and a dash of humor. No longer a hunting dog, he has found a place in the homes and hearts of people all over the world. As evidence, consider that Boxers have been in the top 20 American Kennel Club (AKC)-registered breeds for most of the past 60 years.

PHYSICAL CHARACTERISTICS

The Boxer we know today looks much like the Boxer of 1920. Before the 20th century, Boxers were stocky, heavy-bodied dogs with a thick square head. After the German breed club formed and defined the standard, owners began to breed for the characteristics they desired. Once established, the Boxer has looked much the same through the decades, encompassing more than 30 generations of dogs.

BODY

The initial impression of a Boxer is one of beauty and athleticism. The American Boxer Club (ABC) describes him as "the well-developed middleweight athlete of dogdom." The breed standard describes the ideal Boxer as set forth by the ABC. Show dogs must conform to this standard and are evaluated in comparison to it.

The initial impression of a Boxer is one of beauty and athleticism.

Although muscled, a Boxer is graceful and not heavy-looking. Viewed from the side he is square, meaning the length from his chest to the point of his upper thigh is roughly the same as the height from the withers (shoulders) to the floor. Boxers have a deep chest that reaches down to their elbows. The bottom line of the stomach tucks up toward the rear, which contributes to his elegant, athletic profile.

Males are 23 to 25 inches (58.5 to 63.5 cm) at the withers, sturdy and big boned when compared to females. Females are 21.5 to 23.5 inches (54.5 to 59.5 cm) and are more delicate. Weight ranges from 50 pounds (22.5 kg) (a small female) to 80 pounds (36 kg) (a large male).

HEAD

A Boxer's most distinctive feature is his finely chiseled head. His muzzle is broad and short. The lower jaw protrudes beyond the upper jaw with a slight upward curve. This contributes to his smoosh-nosed appearance, referred to as "brachycephalic." (Other brachycephalic breeds include Bulldogs, Boston Terriers, and Pugs.) The Boxer's nose is set back and slightly high. This unique facial structure actually had a purpose in early Boxers: It allowed them to breathe while holding onto prey with their powerful jaws. Their upper lips fall over the lower lips but do not cover the lower jaw in front.

The Boxer muzzle and nose are always black, and there are folds beneath his eyes that continue to the bottom of his flews (upper lips). The folds shouldn't be too deep because extreme wrinkles hold moisture, which encourages infection.

EARS

Boxer ears may be either left natural or cropped. Ears are set at the highest points of the sides of the skull. Natural ears stand up slightly at the base and fold over.

The upright portion of the ear gives the Boxer's face a square look. The top of the head seems to be almost level with the fold in the ears. Many people feel that natural ears give the Boxer a friendlier expression than cropped ears.

If cropping is decided upon, it is done when a pup is six to nine weeks old. This is a surgical procedure performed by a veterinarian while the dog is under anesthesia. The ears are cut so that they stand upright and are long and tapered at the end. After surgery, the ears need daily care to prevent infection. Once the stitches are removed, the ears must be taped and braced for three to five months so that they stand up properly.

Although cropped ears contribute to the Boxer's alert expression, there is no practical need for this surgery. In the 19th century, owners cropped their Boxers' ears to prevent them from being torn off or injured while their dogs were hunting or fighting. In the days before regular veterinary care was common, upright ears were also less likely to become infected.

Natural ears stand up slightly at the base and fold over, giving the Boxer a friendly expression.

EXPRESSION

A Boxer's expression will melt your heart. He is extremely sensitive to his owner's moods, whether you are nervous, afraid, or deliriously happy. His deep brown eyes and wrinkled forehead, combined with a comical tilt of his head, let you know that he understands everything you just said to him and that he shares your feelings completely. The famous "Boxer smile" is almost human.

COAT AND COLORS

A Boxer's coat is short, shiny, and smooth, described in the breed standard as "held tight to his body." Although you'd think Boxers wouldn't lose much hair, they do shed some throughout the year.

Boxers are one of three colors: brindle, fawn, or white. All three colors often appear in one litter. Color has no effect on a Boxer's temperament. Colored Boxers often have flashy white markings: some combination of a white blaze, white collar, chest, or feet. A plain dog with no white is equally acceptable, and in the early days of the breed, was preferred.

Brindle

A brindle dog has broken black stripes over a fawn background. Brindling varies from almost none to so heavy that the dog appears almost black, called reverse brindle.

Fawn

About 25 percent of all Boxers are born white or mostly white.

Fawn ranges from light tan to a deep mahogany red and is the most common color.

White

About 25 percent of all Boxers are born white or mostly white. Although white Boxers have existed since the mid-1800s, they have never been favored in the show ring. White Boxers are now recognized as being of an acceptable color, and they make wonderful pets. Some dogs are white with large patches of brindle or fawn, referred to as "check" or "parti-colored." Any Boxer who is more than one-third white is sold with a limited registration. He is still AKC registered but cannot be bred or shown. Any puppies produced cannot be registered.

A small percentage of white Boxers are deaf in one or both ears. This is related to a lack of pigment in the ear canal. Deafness also occurs in white dogs of other breeds—for instance, Dalmatians and Shetland Sheepdogs. White Boxers are also susceptible to sunburn and skin cancer.

Other Colors?

In the early years of the breed there were a few black Boxers, but the color never caught on, and selective breeding eliminated them after WWI. When you see what appears to be a black Boxer today, close examination will reveal that he is a reverse brindle.

Beware of breeders selling "rare" blue Boxers, which are either mixed breeds or a genetically dilute color. They are not more valuable.

TAILS AND DEWCLAWS

Since the earliest days of the Bullenbeisser, owners docked their dogs' tails because while hunting or fighting their long, thin tail could easily break. Today's breeders continue the custom, cutting tails short when pups are three to five days old. Front dewclaws are removed at the same time. Boxers are not born with rear dewclaws.

The Boxer's greatest desire is for human affection and company.

LIVING WITH A BOXER

The Boxer is described as a "hearing guard dog" because hearing is his strongest sense. He is instinctively alert and vigilant but not nervous. His intelligence and high energy sometimes overwhelm new owners. Curious and tenacious, he'll stick with an investigation until he is sure that he knows what's going on and is reassured that the world is safe for his family. He is wary and aloof with strangers—

Dog Tale

Peggy Weiss tells about her Boxer Satch, whom she owned when she was in school:
"Once he followed me to the movie theater. I thought he would just wait or get tired and go home, which was only three blocks away. About 30 minutes into the movie, I heard this jingle-jingle. I knew it was him; how he found me in a theater full of kids, I don't know. Well, this was a good movie and I didn't want to miss it, so I called a cab and sent him home. My mother laughed when she saw him arrive in the backseat of the cab."

he'll make quite a racket and intimidate even the most dog-savvy guests. Once satisfied that they are not a threat, though, he'll quickly accept his new best friends.

More intriguing and challenging to own than some other breeds, Boxers are not always the best choice for a first-time dog owner. The breed has been described as a gentle guard dog, dominant without the aggression seen in other guarding breeds. He needs an owner who provides active leadership and keeps up his training and socialization.

COMPANIONABILITY

Boxers are more interested in people than in other dogs. Their greatest desire is for human affection and company. Their urge to be with their humans every minute annoys some people and delights others. Your Boxer will follow your every step around the house and wait outside the bathroom door for you. And when you retire to the couch for the evening, he'll climb into your lap and cover you in wet, slobbery kisses.

Although wary with strangers, Boxers are loyal and devoted to family members, especially children. Not a one-person dog, a Boxer will have a unique relationship with each member of the family. Frau Stockmann, in her book *My Life With Boxers*, wrote decades ago: "His real job is to be a house and family dog and to be a friend to the children." That is still true today.

Your Boxer may be slow to warm up to other dogs and won't back down if aggressively challenged.

With Children

Boxers have a special bond with children. They are famous for protectively watching over "their" kids. They tolerate a lot of handling and seem to know that they need to play gently. But Boxers are also sturdy dogs and enjoy roughhousing. They jump a lot and box with their front paws, unaware of their strength. Supervise rambunctious play and step in if it gets too rough.

Teach your children that if the dog is playing too hard, they should stand still and hold their arms at their sides without looking at him. Running and flailing around (something all kids do) only encourage a dog to nip and jump. If kids settle down, the dog will settle down too.

Your Boxer will appreciate a no-kids zone, like his crate, where he can get away when he's had enough. Your children must respect him and give him space when he needs it. They should learn never to bother him when he is sleeping or eating. (And just a note: Don't let your kids feed the dog from the table or you'll have an incurable canine beggar on your hands.)

Even a well-mannered Boxer has his limits. If a child hits or pinches too hard, a dog disciplines in the only way he knows how: with his teeth. It's the dog who suffers for this mistake, ending up euthanized for acting like a dog.

With Other Dogs

A Boxer is not a Labrador or Golden Retriever, breeds that joyously greet every new dog like a long-lost friend. Your Boxer may be slow to warm up to other dogs and won't back down if aggressively challenged. Boxers are not always the best dogs to take to the dog park. Prevent conflicts by exposing your Boxer to other dogs and people often throughout his life. If he has positive experiences, he'll be much less likely to act defensively.

That being said, many Boxers get along with dogs of all breeds and never have a problem. One of my favorite photos is of a pile of Boxers lying in a tangle of legs, with one sitting on another's head. Two males or a male and a female are most likely to get along. Unaltered dogs are the most likely to fight. Rather than bring a strange dog into your home, introduce them on neutral territory.

With Other Pets

If your Boxer grows up with cats, they may become fast friends. However, his high prey drive may kick in when he meets an unfamiliar kitty or other pet. Small pets and livestock like guinea pigs, rabbits, and chickens are safer when kept separate from the Boxer in the household.

MALE AND FEMALE TEMPERAMENT

Males are the clowns of the Boxer world. More easily distracted than females, they take longer to train than females. They are also very sensitive, never forgetting an insult or harsh correction.

Females are more independent and serious. They'll check in with you regularly but won't be underfoot as much as a male. Females have been described as caregivers, thoughtful and gentle with everyone. One owner told me about her young Boxer who took care of the family's deaf and blind Boston Terrier. She constantly stayed by the Boston's side and gently helped him find his way around the house and yard.

ENVIRONMENT

Boxers are adaptable and quickly adjust to almost any home. As long as they are indoors with you, they are happy. Some environments meet the breed's needs better than others, but wherever they live, Boxers require a yard and a daily exercise plan, especially when they are young.

Rural

Boxers do well in a rural setting but should never be allowed to run loose. A

Boxers are adaptable and quickly adjust to almost any home.

secure fenced dog run or yard is a must. On his own, a Boxer will expand the territory he feels responsible for and become overprotective. He'll also chase the neighbors' animals. In the country, some people shoot stray dogs who chase their livestock. Skunks and other wildlife encounters are also a danger.

Tying him out on a chain is not an option. Dogs instinctively respond by fleeing from something that scares them. Because a tied-up dog can't escape, he has to defend himself from every perceived threat. Gradually he'll become aggressive as he tries to fend off "intruders" before they get to him. He'll also become frustrated because he can't get to his people and other animals.

Suburban

A family home in the suburbs is an excellent environment for a Boxer. Be sure that you have a solid fence so that he doesn't bark at passersby. Once he is past the destructive phase, the ideal setup is a dog door where he can go in and out as he wishes.

Urban

An apartment or condo is not the best home for a Boxer, but if you have an active lifestyle and he goes along with you on outings, a committed owner can make it work. A crate is your best friend when you have to leave him at home.

EXERCISE REQUIREMENTS

Boxers have tremendous energy and require at least an hour of hard exercise every day. They make great jogging or hiking partners. If you slack off, your Boxer will become destructive and develop an assortment of problem behaviors. If you work all day, consider doggy day care or hire a dog walker. During cold winter months, owners take their dogs for short romps in the snow or set up indoor games. Toss a ball up and down the stairs while he chases it. Exercise him on a treadmill.

Mental exercise is important too. Treat dispensers and puzzle toys entertain a restless dog. Play hide-and-seek with treats, or have him search for you. Competitive dog sports and training sessions exercise his mind as well as his body.

PERSONALITY

Boxers are social, playful, and always active, and every day is a new adventure when you own one. Peggy Weiss of Missouri sums up the Boxer's outlook on life: "You know, if people woke up in the morning happy and playful like these Boxers, it would be a better world. Every morning, mine greets me all licks and wiggling butt like he hasn't seen me in six months."

You can't talk about Boxer temperament without noting the breed's sense of humor. Be careful what you laugh at because the slightest giggle turns him into a

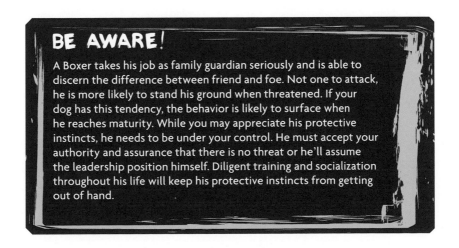

BE AWARE!

A Boxer takes his job as family guardian seriously and is able to discern the difference between friend and foe. Not one to attack, he is more likely to stand his ground when threatened. If your dog has this tendency, the behavior is likely to surface when he reaches maturity. While you may appreciate his protective instincts, he needs to be under your control. He must accept your authority and assurance that there is no threat or he'll assume the leadership position himself. Diligent training and socialization throughout his life will keep his protective instincts from getting out of hand.

complete ham. His physical contortions appear to bend him in half like a kidney bean when he's happy. He doesn't just wag his tail—he wags his entire body with delight when he realizes that he has successfully entertained you.

One owner, Tracy Hendrickson of Texas, told me about staying at a hotel with her three Boxers. The door somehow opened while she was out. When she returned, all three were romping around in the hallway. Mortified, she made sure that she shut the door carefully the next time she went out. She came back to find her female Boxer outside the door, working the knob in her mouth until she opened it so that she could go back into the room.

TRAINABILITY

Over the past century Boxers have served as assistance dogs for the disabled, police dogs, military dogs, and therapy dogs. Many owners compete in obedience, agility, and other canine sports. All this is proof that Boxers can be trained, despite what some people might tell you. One person described it this way:

"The difference between a Border Collie and a Boxer is that if you train a Border Collie to go to the store by taking him down to the corner, waiting for the light, and crossing in the crosswalk, he'll learn to do exactly that. The Boxer will just cross the street and get to the store."

Boxers are social, playful, and always active.

A well-trained Boxer is a loyal and faithful friend for life.

Having said that, I have to say that the truth is that Boxers are trainable but not necessarily easy to train. They were developed to work alone, as sentries, messengers, and hunters. Thus they are independent thinkers. They want to know why you are asking them to do something. The Boxer is a natural problem solver and loves to work out his own solutions, but they might not be the same solutions you had in mind. And if you dare laugh at his antics he'll offer the same trick again and again, with a mischievous sparkle in his eyes. Boxers take a long time to mature and aren't really adults until they are two years old, so they need persistent and consistent training. If you give them an inch, they'll take a mile!

Your Boxer's acute sense of hearing means that he is aware of everything around him and is easily distracted. He'll use this as an excuse to distract you from training him. To counteract this, make training a game and use lots of rewards.

Boxers learn quickly and love to be with their owners. Once your dog knows that it's time to work, he'll settle down and enjoy the challenge. He'll look forward to your time together and work hard to earn your approval. Because Boxers are so sensitive to your emotions, the slightest verbal correction is often the most effective. Harsh treatment will only ruin your relationship.

Training is a lifelong project with any dog. It also develops your bond with him. Involve the entire family so that he responds equally well to everyone. You'll be glad that you did. A well-trained Boxer is a loyal and faithful friend for life.

SUPPLIES FOR YOUR BOXER

The well-dressed Boxer needs some basic supplies to keep him happy, healthy, and well fed. Boxers are not large dogs, so you don't need to super-size the items you buy for yours. Invest in easy-care, washable, and fairly indestructible items, at least until he's old enough to take care of his possessions.

BED

I don't think there is such a thing as a chew-proof dog bed. Save some money and buy cheap substitutes at garage sales, at least in the beginning. Beds don't need to be elaborate; a simple throw rug or an old blanket provides a soft spot to sleep. Teach your Boxer to relax on his bed when he's indoors. He'll soon learn to go there when you don't want him in the midst of activities. When you board him, take his bed along to the kennel so that he'll have something familiar that reminds him of home.

Once you are ready to invest in a real bed, there are many choices. A wicker bed is one, but they are not practical if your dog is a chewer, so choose a more durable bed. Plush pillows come in a variety of styles: bolster edges, flat slabs, beanbags, and donuts. They are filled with polyester fiberfill, foam rubber, or cedar chips in a muslin liner. Cedar helps to repel fleas and combat odors. Beds for senior dogs are often filled with egg-crate foam to cushion aching joints.

Check to be sure the covers are removable and washable. I find that Boxers like a bed with high sides that seem too small. They curl up in a tiny ball, spilling out over the edge.

Because Boxers are so susceptible to heat exhaustion, consider cooling beds for summer use. Outdoor beds are covered with waterproof material similar to patio cushions. Made with a PVC pipe or metal frame and raised above the ground, they allow air circulation on a hot day. They're also easy to clean—just hose them down and let them air-dry. Another hot-weather option is cooler pads, which you fill with cold water and refrigerate. Use them indoors, outdoors, or in a crate.

For fun, go the luxury route and buy small couches or beds covered in designer fabric, faux fur, or leather. There is no limit to how much money you can spend to pamper your pooch!

Teach your Boxer to relax on his bed when he's indoors.

COLLAR

Collars come in an endless array of styles and colors.

Here's your opportunity to make a fashion statement. Collars come in an endless array of styles and colors. Most people choose a flat buckle or snap closure style in leather or nylon. Many Boxer owners like rolled leather collars because they don't rub the coat the way a flat collar does.

A martingale collar solves the problem of having a dog pull out of his collar and take off running. A martingale fits over the dog's head without a buckle opening. A loop tightens and prevents him from backing out of it when he pulls on the leash. The rest of the time the collar hangs loose.

Not recommended for most Boxers: a head halter, which fits on the dog's muzzle like a horse's halter. The leash attaches to a ring under his jaw. For many Boxers, their muzzles are just too short for halters to stay on properly. You also risk injuring your dog's eyes with the strap that goes over his nose.

CRATE

A Boxer loves a cozy place to curl up and take a nap. Don't think of a crate as punishment or a jail. Your dog doesn't see it that way.

Choose a crate that is big enough for him to stand up and turn around but not so big that he has room to eliminate. If you are just starting to crate train, buy a sturdy one that he can't destroy. Thin wire, flimsy plastic, or fabric crates won't hold up to a determined escape artist.

There are several kinds of crates:

Fabric or Mesh

These are often made of waterproof fabrics that can be hosed down outdoors when dirty. Lightweight, collapsible, and easy to transport, they are convenient for family outings or dog shows. Many styles have pockets on the sides for storing treats, leashes, and other necessities. If your Boxer is not yet crate trained, he'll probably destroy it. Train him with another type of crate first.

Plastic

Airlines require that dogs travel in heavy-duty plastic crates. Check with the carrier for its requirements before you buy. Most crates are labeled if they are approved for shipping.

Wire

These are convenient for home use because they fold up and store easily. Air circulates better than in a plastic crate, so our heat-sensitive Boxers are safer. When it is cold, cover the crate with a blanket (also a good way to get him to settle down

PUPPY POINTER

Many wire crates have a moveable panel that blocks a section until a puppy grows up. This helps with his housetraining; he won't want to eliminate where he sleeps. He'll also feel safer and more secure in a confined space. And you won't have to buy another crate when he gets bigger!

and stop barking). A wire crate often has a door on the side as well as on one end, which gives you the option to arrange it to fit your room. Prices vary dramatically because of different gauges of wire and quality of construction. Choose something sturdy enough that it lasts.

Wood Crates or Crate Covers

Coordinate your dog's decor with your own. For the fashion conscious, you don't have to have an ugly crate cluttering up your home. Purchase wood crates or crate covers that slip over wire crates. They make a lovely end table.

CRATE PADS

Keep your dog comfortable by providing washable pads sized to fit the crate. But he will be fine without a pad if you think that he'll chew it. Teenaged dogs are most likely to chew their beds; puppies often like something warm to snuggle with.

DOGHOUSE

Boxers aren't happy spending their lives outdoors, away from their humans. But if yours has to be outside for a short period, a doghouse will keep him cozy and safe. Face the door away from direct sunlight and wind. The floor should be elevated off wet ground. His house shouldn't be too big—just large enough for him to turn around. A doghouse that is too big won't hold his body heat.

DOG RUN

If you don't have a fenced yard, add a covered dog run to your supply list. I advise a cover for two reasons: 1.) Dogs need protection from sun, rain, and snow, and 2.) bored Boxers climb fences, so a roof keeps them confined.

Purchase a chain link run at a home center, pet supply store, or feed store. They are available in an assortment of sizes. The dog needs enough room in which to relieve himself without having to lie in his waste. If you get a portable run, anchor it to solid posts that are cemented into the ground. Otherwise, a strong dog can work his way under the fence panels.

Add a doghouse for extra protection from the weather. Don't forget that he needs a water bowl or bucket as well.

If you live in an area with extreme weather, consider installing the dog run in your garage or basement. That way your Boxer gets to be indoors but is not as confined as if he had to stay in a crate.

EXERCISE PEN

When a baby is old enough to crawl, she must be watched every second or confined to a playpen. For a young Boxer, an exercise pen, or ex-pen, is the canine equivalent of the playpen. Without constant supervision, he'll become a one-dog destruction derby. An ex-pen helps you get through that stage with less damage.

Ex-pens are usually 24 to 36 inches (61 to 91.5 cm) tall and made out of wire mesh. For Boxers, I recommend the taller one. If introduced to it while still a pup, your Boxer will accept the ex-pen without trying to escape. He won't be as confined as when he is in a crate and will still get to be where all the action is. Put him into his pen with a snack-filled chew toy while you are eating dinner, when company comes, or at other times when you don't want him underfoot. An adult Boxer who isn't familiar with an ex-pen will probably jump right out and go about his business, so you are better off using a crate.

Ex-pens are also handy to take along when you travel. They fold flat for easy transport.

Dog Tale

Tucker and Tyson are typical Boxers when it comes to toys. Their owner's girlfriend, Kathy, bought the dogs an "indestructible" stuffed animal for Christmas. She searched hard to find a toy that was well made and would really last. Within ten minutes the squeaky was removed and the stuffing was all over the house. But the head was still stuffed, and months later they still carry it around by the head playing toss and catch.

FOOD AND WATER BOWLS

A food bowl does not need to be huge because you will probably never feed your Boxer more than 2 or 3 cups at a time. Most dog bowls make great toys, so expect your Boxer's dishes to take some serious abuse. Stainless steel bowls are relatively indestructible and discourage the most determined chewer. A rubber-bottomed steel bowl doesn't scoot across the floor as your dog eats. Plastic bowls are hard to clean if your Boxer chews on them and also won't last as long. Ceramic bowls are heavy and hard to pick up, but if broken your dog might get cut. Ant-proof bowls have a reservoir (like a moat) around the main bowl. Fill the moat with soapy water to keep the ants out of dog food.

Experts recommend that you feed your dog at floor level. Deep-chested dogs like the Boxer are at risk for bloat, an emergency condition in which the stomach fills with gas and twists. A dog is more likely to gulp air, which is a cause of bloat, while eating from a raised bowl. (For more information on this condition, see Chapter 6.)

For a dog who plays in his water bowl outdoors, a metal bucket that clips to the fence will prevent him from spilling it or at least slow him down. Or purchase a nozzle that attaches to your outdoor faucet. The dog licks it and gets fresh clean water every time. It takes a little training to get him to understand it, but once he does you won't have to worry about spills or dirty water bowls.

A rubber-bottomed steel bowl is best for your Boxer because it won't move across the floor as he eats.

GROOMING SUPPLIES

Even the wash-and-wear Boxer needs a few basic grooming supplies. Start with a grooming glove, rubber currycomb, toenail clippers, dog shampoo, and canine toothpaste and toothbrush. (See Chapter 5 for information on how to use these tools.)

IDENTIFICATION

Your Boxer should have two types of identification: an ID tag and a microchip.

ID TAG

An identification tag is essential for every Boxer. If your dog is lost and ends up in a shelter, especially far from home, he could be euthanized before you find him.

Plastic tags break apart after a year or so, so invest in engraved metal and include your name and phone number. Consider adding your cell phone number and e-mail address on his tag as well.

If you hate the sound of jingling tags, order a collar with your phone number printed on the fabric. Tag covers or pouches that attach to the collar are also available.

MICROCHIP

A microchip is injected under your Boxer's skin between the shoulder blades. It is encoded with an ID number that is registered in a national database. Smaller than a grain of rice, it is encased in surgical glass to prevent infection. A microchip is beneficial because if your dog loses his collar he can still be identified. Whoever finds him can locate you before it is too late.

There are many brands of microchips. In recent years, universal ISO-compliant (International Organization for Standardization) scanners have been developed that read all brands and frequencies. Wherever in the world your dog is found, you can be reunited.

When a shelter worker runs a scanner over the dog, the number appears, just as a grocery store scanner reads the code on a product label. That number is then entered in the database and you are contacted.

Once your dog is microchipped, you pay a one-time fee to a national registry. It keeps your information on file and updated for the life of the dog. The vet provides registration information when you have the chip implanted. Shelters, rescue groups, and pet supply stores also offer microchipping.

A microchip can sometimes migrate to a dog's shoulder or leg. Have your vet scan him during his annual checkup to be sure that the chip is still in place.

LEASH

I recommend leather leashes because they are soft and easy on your hands. A flat nylon leash will burn your hands if your dog pulls hard. I recommend a 4-foot (1-m) leash, although some people prefer a 6-foot (2-m) leash. You don't really need 6 feet (2 m), though, and if your dog walks that far away from you he is likely to start pulling. If you do choose a longer leash, gather up some of the length while walking.

Retractable leashes extend from 12 to 16 feet (3.5 to 5 m) and allow a dog more leeway to explore. Again, these are great as long as he is not a puller. One downside: he'll yank the bulky handle out of your hand if he decides to chase something.

If you worry about injuring your dog's neck because he pulls, there are a variety of no-pull harnesses available. Made with movable straps that thread under a dog's front legs and up under his armpits, these harnesses fasten to the leash either between

Leather leashes are soft and easy on the hands.

the shoulder blades or on the chest. When he pulls, it corrects him. But if you teach your dog to walk nicely on a leash, you won't need any fancy devices. (See Chapter 7.)

LICENSE

Most areas require a city or county license once a dog is a few months old. Animal control agencies notify the owner when a licensed dog is picked up and hold him longer than they would a nonlicensed dog.

Licenses cost less if the dog is spayed or neutered. Some licenses are good for several years, and some must be renewed annually.

PET GATE

A pet gate is indispensable when you are training a Boxer, young or old. It's easier to supervise (and housetrain) your dog if you limit his access to portions of the house. If introduced to the gate while young, he'll be less likely to jump over it when he grows up. My experience has been that even adult Boxers who have never seen a pet gate honor the boundary.

Twenty-four- to 36-inch-tall (61- to 91.5-cm) pressure-mounted gates are inexpensive. They also don't permanently damage your doorway with mounting hardware. I suggest the taller one; no reason to tempt your Boxer. They come in adjustable widths for different doors, up to 48 inches (122 cm). Choose one with a finger-trigger latch so that you can open the gate with one hand. If you'd like to keep the barrier up permanently, consider a fancier gate that coordinates with your decor.

For wider openings, decorative freestanding gates/fences serve to block access.

SWEATER

If you live in a cold climate, consider a sweater or two for your canine companion. Boxers don't have a thick coat to protect them during walks or while playing in the snow. (You should never leave your Boxer outside in extreme cold.) A friend of mine in the Northwest also has a rain slicker for her Boxer.

TOYS

Boxers love a good game, and nothing is more fun than pouncing on a stuffed animal and shredding it to bits. With that in mind, some toys are okay to leave out, but some need to be put away when you're not there to supervise. Once you get to know your dog's chewing habits, you'll be able to decide which toys are safest.

Because Boxers love to chew, choose heavy-duty toys. Many rubber bones and so-called chew toys break up quickly. My favorite indestructible toy is the Galileo bone, which lasts for months. Empty plastic water jugs are free, entertaining, and capable of making lots of fun noise. Just throw them away when your Boxer starts to chew them.

Boxers also enjoy heavy rope toys made with fine string and knotted at the ends. They'll sling them around in the air, chasing and pouncing on them. Throw these toys away when the rope starts to come apart because big chunks can block the digestive tract.

Boxers need mental exercise as well as physical. Interactive puzzle toys entertain your dog while feeding him. Fill food-dispensing toys with his kibble or treats and he'll push the toy around to release the goodies. You'll need to show him how to get to the treats at first, but once he figures it out he'll enjoy the challenge. In multiple-dog homes, these toys might cause a fight, so they are best for an only dog.

Fill hollow rubber chew toys with peanut butter, cheese, or liver sausage. Extend their life by freezing the stuffed toy. It will take your dog longer to dig out the goodies.

To keep toys fresh and new in your Boxer's eyes, rotate his collection by hiding some for a few days.

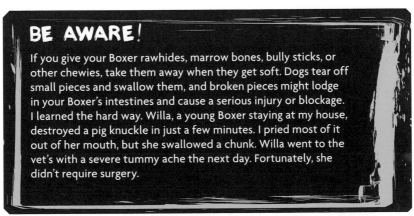

BE AWARE!

If you give your Boxer rawhides, marrow bones, bully sticks, or other chewies, take them away when they get soft. Dogs tear off small pieces and swallow them, and broken pieces might lodge in your Boxer's intestines and cause a serious injury or blockage. I learned the hard way. Willa, a young Boxer staying at my house, destroyed a pig knuckle in just a few minutes. I pried most of it out of her mouth, but she swallowed a chunk. Willa went to the vet's with a severe tummy ache the next day. Fortunately, she didn't require surgery.

FEEDING
YOUR BOXER

We all want to choose the healthiest food for our Boxers, but there is no one perfect diet for every dog. Your dog's individual needs dictate which food is best for him. Once you understand the basics, the endless choices won't seem like such a challenge.

The American Association of Feed Control Officials (AAFCO) establishes standards for minimum and maximum levels of certain nutrients in pet food. Even so, all foods are not the same. Manufacturers use different ingredients to meet the standards, and expensive food is not necessarily better.

So how do you tell which food is best? My opinion has always been: If it works, don't fix it. There is no reason to change food if your dog has a healthy skin and coat, clear eyes, clean ears, consistent digestive function, and plenty of energy.

BASIC NUTRITION

The major nutrients in a healthy balanced canine diet are carbohydrates, fats, minerals, proteins, vitamins, and water. Each contributes to overall body function in a different way.

CARBOHYDRATES

Dogs do not absolutely require carbohydrates in their diet, but they have been eating carbs since mankind began feeding dogs. Although they get the protein and fat they need from meat, carbs provide many benefits.

Carbohydrates are a source of glucose, which provides energy.

Carbohydrates are a source of glucose, which provides energy. Simple carbohydrates (e.g., fruit) are easily absorbed by the body and convert to glucose. Complex carbs (e.g., grains, potatoes, and peas and beans) provide starches and dietary fiber, which help the digestive system function properly. Starches are also essential to dry food processing, giving the food structure and texture.

Whole grains (e.g., oatmeal, whole wheat) are a healthy source of carbohydrates, dietary fiber, B vitamins, and minerals. Refined grains (e.g., white flour, brewer's rice, wheat bran) are stripped of dietary fiber, iron, and B vitamins. They provide minimal nutrition but the same number of calories. The body quickly digests refined grains, providing glucose, so they aren't totally useless. Empty carbs, also called fillers (e.g., cellulose, beet pulp, peanut hulls) have no nutritional value and are added to provide extra fiber. While they offer no nutritional benefit, they help the contents of the bowel travel through the gut and form into a solid stool. These poor-quality fiber sources are harder to digest and may contribute to excess gas.

Grains are less expensive than meat, and many dogs thrive on grain-based foods. They are perfectly acceptable unless a dog's medical issues indicate a need to

Essential fatty acids contribute to the Boxer's coat quality and help lubricate his joints.

change. However, there has been a trend in recent years to switch dogs to a grain-free diet for an assortment of reasons:

- Grain allergies, especially to corn, are often a problem for Boxers.
- Low-carbohydrate diets are often recommended for dogs suffering from obesity, diabetes, pancreatitis, or cancer.
- Grains are sometimes harder to digest for a dog with stomach issues. Low fiber puts less stress on the gut. At the same time, high-fiber diets help solidify the stool and prevent diarrhea.
- There is evidence that cereal grain carbohydrates, often used as a protein source in dog food, contribute to hyperactivity. Boxers are naturally energetic, but you might see a difference if you switch to a diet that is higher in animal protein sources.

A grain-free diet is not necessarily a carbohydrate-free diet. Ingredients such as potatoes, peas, beans, apples, and sweet potatoes also supply carbohydrates.

FATS

Fats supply a highly concentrated form of energy, providing more than either proteins or carbohydrates. They also provide the fat-soluble vitamins A, D, E, and K, as well as essential fatty acids. Essential fatty acids contribute to coat quality and help lubricate joints. Dogs with high energy requirements need more fat, and obese dogs need much less. Usually sprayed onto kibble after cooking, fats also add taste and texture to dry food.

MINERALS

Minerals are essential to healthy bones and teeth and help maintain electrolyte and fluid balance. Calcium is probably the most well-known mineral, and a deficiency quickly causes tooth loss, broken bones, and anemia. Calcium and phosphorus affect hormone levels and body functions like muscle contraction. Other important minerals affect a variety of body functions, for example: copper (red blood cell production), iodine (thyroid function), magnesium (carbohydrate metabolization), selenium (strengthens the immune system), and zinc (digestion).

PROTEINS

Protein manufactures glucose and energy, which are required for all cellular functions. Excess energy not used by the body is either stored as fat or excreted in urine and feces. Protein is also the source of essential amino acids and nitrogen, and it is necessary for healthy muscles, bones, skin, and hair. A dog with a protein deficiency has muscle wasting, a dull coat, poor growth, and weight loss.

Dogs are omnivorous, meaning they eat both plants and animals. Meat, fish, and poultry are high-quality sources of protein and are more digestible than plant proteins. Manufacturers often use plant proteins such as corn or wheat gluten because they are less expensive than animal proteins.

Meat appears in several forms in dog food, and the differences are important indicators of quality. The specific source of the meat should be named, such as beef, lamb, or chicken, unless several sources are used. Meat "meal" has the water removed and therefore provides more nutrients per pound (.5 kg) than fresh meat. The AAFCO defines meat "by-products" as nonrendered parts of mammals that do not include meat—for example, bone, blood, and various organs.

Exotic protein sources, such as bison, venison, and duck, are often used in premium foods. It's not necessary to buy these expensive foods unless your dog has a proven sensitivity to beef or chicken, the most commonly used meats.

VITAMINS

Vitamins provide antioxidants and enzymes that help cells function. Dogs can't manufacture enough vitamins to meet their daily needs, so food manufacturers add them in small amounts. You should not need to supplement a nutritionally complete commercial food with additional vitamins.

Vitamins fall into two categories. Fat-soluble vitamins (A, D, E, and K) are stored in the liver, and excess is toxic. Water-soluble vitamins (assorted B vitamins and vitamin C) are flushed out in the urine, and excess is not as risky.

Poor storage, heat, humidity, fat rancidity, and oxidation all affect the vitamin content in dog food. Check the expiration date on the package when you purchase it to ensure that the food is fresh.

WATER

An adult dog's body is almost 60 percent moisture. Dehydration kills a dog faster than starvation; without water, our dogs could not survive. You may not think of it as a nutrient, but lack of water causes a host of health problems, including constipation and organ failure. Be sure that your dog has access to clean, fresh water. He won't want to drink out of a dirty, algae-covered dish.

THE FEEDING ROUTINE

Boxers do best on two or even three meals a day. Feeding several smaller meals limits the risk of bloat, a condition in which the stomach fills with gas and twists. Boxers are highly susceptible to this sometimes-fatal illness. (See Chapter 6.) Soak his food in water so that it expands in the bowl, not in his stomach.

Put the food down, and if he hasn't finished it in ten minutes, pick up the bowl and save it for the next meal. Here's why:

- Free-feeding, where the food is down all day, makes it harder for you to monitor how much your dog is eating (or not eating). You could miss signs of illness.
- As the food provider, you are the leader in your Boxer's eyes.
- Some Boxers are picky eaters, and food has more value if it isn't readily available.
- Food that is left out attracts insects like ants.
- Regular meals help with housetraining because he is on a predictable schedule.

Be sure that your Boxer has access to clean, fresh water.

HOW MUCH TO FEED

The American Animal Hospital Association (AAHA) states that the appropriate amount of food varies by as much as 30 percent more or less than what is recommended on the bag. Take into consideration your Boxer's age, amount of daily exercise, overall health, and the type of food you are feeding. Don't forget to count treats and table scraps—they have calories too.

If you are feeding a premium brand of food made with high-quality ingredients, feed smaller meals. Your Boxer's body absorbs the nutrients more efficiently and produces smaller stools.

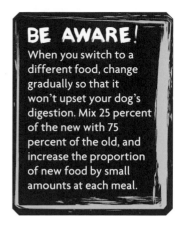

BE AWARE!
When you switch to a different food, change gradually so that it won't upset your dog's digestion. Mix 25 percent of the new with 75 percent of the old, and increase the proportion of new food by small amounts at each meal.

PICKY EATING

It's not going to kill your dog to miss a meal, but some owners tear their hair out trying to get their Boxer to eat. If he's not underweight, don't worry if he skips breakfast. He'll eat at the next meal. It is not unusual for a dog to fast for a day. Monitor his stools for diarrhea or other stomach upset that might require veterinary attention.

To make your dog's meal more palatable, add a little water or some canned food. Don't let him train you to feed him table scraps and human food exclusively. Of course he's going to prefer that!

COMMERCIAL FOODS

All dog foods are not created equal. Although they are required to contain certain nutrients, the specific ingredients and quality vary among brands and sometimes even from batch to batch within the same brand. It's up to you to decide which one works best for your Boxer.

The United States Department of Agriculture (USDA) requires that manufacturers list the ingredients and nutrients used to make up their food. Green or orange bits in a dog's food aren't necessarily vegetables. Gums and coloring are used to bind ingredients together and make the food look appealing to consumers. Pictures of raw meat, fruits, and vegetables are on the label to convince you, the owner, to purchase their brand. The fine print is where you really find out what's in that bag.

The USDA and Food and Drug Administration (FDA) specifically outlines the wording that must be used to define certain types of foods. Even the name of the food is strictly regulated. When a food is named "chicken," for example, 95 percent of the ingredients (excluding water) must be chicken. On the other hand, "chicken dinner," "recipe," or "formula" has to contain only 25 percent chicken. If "with" precedes an ingredient name, for example "with chicken," only 3 percent chicken is required. And "chicken-flavored" food only needs to taste like chicken; there may be no real chicken at all. A food also cannot be labeled "organic" unless it meets specific requirements.

A dog food label should specify the guaranteed analysis of a food.

For a food to be considered "complete and balanced," it must contain the correct percentage of nutrients (per AAFCO standards) for either "adult maintenance," "growth," or "all life stages." There is no specified requirement for senior foods at this time. Pet foods are eligible to use the terminology "complete and balanced" in three different ways:
• by successfully completing a feeding trial (the most reliable method)
• by meeting nutritional minimums and maximum levels as set by the AAFCO (confirmed by laboratory testing)
• through a "family member," meaning that another food in the manufacturer's line of foods passed a feeding trial, and this food is similar in composition

The label also specifies the guaranteed analysis of a food. This list provides the minimum percentages of crude protein and fat and maximum percentages of fiber and moisture. The percentages don't tell you what ingredients make up these nutrients. The actual ingredients are what really determine the quality of the food.

The ingredients list is provided in order from the most to the least. Choose a food that has meat or meat meal listed as the first ingredient. Beware of meat by-products, which are not actually meat. The next four or five ingredients are critical. If two or three out of the next items are grains, it's quite possible that they add up to more grain than meat in the food.

Preservatives must also be listed on the label. They prevent vitamin and fat loss during storage and extend the shelf life of the food once it is opened. Antioxidants, for example, vitamin C and mixed tocopherols (vitamin E), are natural preservatives. Less desirable are the synthetic preservatives ethoxyquin, BHT, or BHA.

DRY FOOD

Commercially manufactured dry food is less expensive and has a longer shelf life than other foods. Dry food varies from inexpensive poor-quality foods that use lots of fillers and cheap protein sources to premium foods that use whole grains and fresh meat. Premium foods contain varied ingredients, so although one food may be more expensive, it is not always the best choice for your particular dog.

Most dry food is extruded, which means that it is steam cooked and the moist ingredients are pushed through a screen to form kibble. Next, the manufacturer sprays on fat, preservatives, and other flavor enhancers that have been destroyed during cooking. Then it is dried to the desired moisture content (usually around 10 percent).

Some dry foods are baked, which is better for dogs who are prone to bloat because it doesn't swell in their stomachs after eating. Baking is more expensive and time consuming, so baked foods are not as common and are usually more expensive.

SEMI-MOIST FOOD

Semi-moist food looks tasty and is often shaped like hamburgers and sausages that appeal to consumers. Even if it looks like hamburger, though, the actual amount of meat varies. These foods are expensive compared to dry and are 25 to 30 percent moisture. High amounts of sucrose (table sugar) are used to bind the product together and prevent spoilage. Sugar is just as bad for your dog's teeth as it is for yours. Semi-moist foods should be served as occasional treats, if at all.

Commercially manufactured dry food is less expensive and has a longer shelf life than other foods.

CANNED FOOD

Canned foods (including those that are packaged in pouches or tubs) are about 78 percent water, which makes your dog feel full faster. They are the most expensive foods but are more palatable because of the higher meat, fat, and water content. Canned food provides higher energy content than dry food and offers other advantages as well. For example, there are fewer preservatives in canned foods because the can is an oxygen-free environment. Once opened, refrigeration prevents spoilage. (Wash your dog's bowl after every meal to prevent bacteria growth and avoid attracting bugs.)

If your older Boxer is not drinking or eating enough, canned food provides additional water, and the smell will entice him to eat. Dogs with bad teeth sometimes have trouble chewing, so canned food ensures that they are getting sufficient nutrition.

Look for food that has a higher percentage of animal protein—whole meat, fish, or poultry—and whole grains and vegetables. Reject brands that use by-products because there is too much variation in ingredients and quality.

Some canned foods are not "complete and balanced," as defined by the AAFCO. Supplement these with dry food to provide the missing nutrients.

NONCOMMERCIAL DIETS

Many Boxer owners successfully feed their dogs raw or home-cooked foods. These diets may benefit a dog who has chronic digestive problems, allergies, or other issues that haven't been solved by traditional medicine. Also, numerous pet food recalls over the past few years have inspired owners to want more control over the quality and safety of their pets' food.

A dog's food must provide the essential nutrients in the right balance, or you'll do more harm than good. Consult with a veterinary nutritionist to develop a complete diet that includes adequate vitamin and mineral supplements. Do plenty of research, but don't believe everything you read on the Internet. Passionate proponents of raw and home-cooked diets have a lot to say

PUPPY POINTER

Long-boned breeds like the Boxer need the higher calcium to phosphorus ratio found in puppy food for proper bone development. Therefore, many Boxer breeders recommend that you feed puppy food until 12 to 18 months of age, when the growth plates (soft areas of growing bone in the hips, knees, and elbows) fuse and harden.

based on personal experience but often don't have the scientific credentials to back up their opinions.

When you switch to a new diet, realize that it takes several months for the full effects, good or bad, to become evident.

Consider these advantages of a raw or home-cooked diet:

- Home-prepared diets don't need preservatives or fillers that have no nutritional value, so dogs with allergies and food sensitivities tend to improve.
- You have complete control over the ingredients, their quality, and freshness. You can also provide variety by taking advantage of seasonal fruits and vegetables.
- You can feed a combination of raw, home-cooked, and commercial food. For example, substitute one meal a day with premium dry or wet food so that your Boxer gets sufficient vitamins and minerals.
- You can experiment until you have a combination of ingredients that works for your dog.

Consider the following disadvantages of a raw or home-cooked diet:

- Research, shopping, preparation, and monitoring your dog's condition are time consuming.
- Ingredients are more expensive than commercial dog food.
- Proper supplementation and achieving a nutritionally balanced diet are challenging. Many home-prepared diets are deficient in calcium, which causes weak bones and dental problems.
- If your dog is eating a raw diet while receiving medication or fighting a disease that causes immune system dysfunction, there is a higher risk he will contract an infection.
- Raw meat carries diseases like salmonella that cause illness in humans. Handle raw meat carefully to prevent contamination.
- Research has shown an increase of disease-causing bacteria carried in the feces of animals fed raw diets.

Here's how to tell if a raw or home-cooked diet is good for your dog:

- Examine your Boxer's stool. Did he absorb the ingredients (good) or did they pass through his system without being digested (not good)?
- Is his coat shiny, with no dandruff or greasiness?
- Are your Boxer's eyes bright and shiny?
- Are his ears clean, or do they smell and look dirty or irritated?
- Are his teeth clean and his gums healthy, or are they red and inflamed?
- Is his energy level appropriate for his age?

HOME-COOKED DIET

Most properly prepared home-cooked dog foods are a mixture of grains, meat, and vegetables combined and cooked slowly into a stew. Remove bones or grind them after cooking because they can splinter in the stomach and perforate the intestine. Cooking depletes vitamins and minerals, so add these vital nutrients based on your vet's recommendation, or add a high-quality dry food to provide the missing nutrients.

A home-cooked diet is not table scraps! Many table scraps provide too much fat and vary so much that they can upset a Boxer's digestion.

RAW DIET

The raw diet movement, also called BARF (Bones and Raw Food), started because some owners feel that it is healthier to feed dogs the way their ancestors ate in the wild. Wolves eat the entire animal, including bones, feet, entrails, and feathers. Proponents believe that this is the way we should feed our dogs today.

Raw bones exercise a dog's teeth and gums and provide calcium. (If you see undigested bone fragments in your dog's stool, grind the bones before

Many Boxer owners successfully feed their dogs raw or home-cooked foods.

feeding to prevent injury.) But although the nutrient content hasn't been altered by cooking, you still have no idea if your dog is getting a proper balance of vitamins and minerals. So whether feeding a cooked or raw diet, you will still have to supplement your Boxer's food. (Check with your vet for advice on how to do so properly.)

Join a raw food co-op to buy in bulk and get wholesale prices. If you are uncomfortable handling raw meat, purchase prepackaged frozen or dehydrated food. Raw has become so popular that even large chains of pet supply stores now carry it. Prepackaged raw food often has vegetables and other ingredients already added.

Most properly prepared home-cooked dog foods are a mixture of grains, meat, and vegetables combined and cooked slowly into a stew.

OBESITY

Boxers are usually lean and muscular. If you run your hands down your dog's sides and can't feel any ribs, he may be too fat. Take a second look. Does his tummy tuck up behind his rib cage? Does he have a waistline when viewed from the top? If not, it's time for a diet.

Visit your veterinarian to evaluate your dog's overall body condition and run tests to rule out illness. Hypothyroidism, for example, often causes weight gain. The doctor may suggest that you switch your dog to a high-fiber, low-calorie food or a prescription diet.

Gradually cut down the amount of food your dog gets each day. If you suddenly reduce the amount, his metabolism will slow down to compensate for the decreased intake. If he's still hungry, add green beans, pumpkin, or other high-fiber vegetables to make him feel full.

Also, cut back on treats. All the healthy meals in the world will do no good if he's gobbling junk food. Carrot bits, sweet potato slices, and regular kibble are healthy rewards. Be sure to subtract any treats from his daily allotment.

Exercise speeds weight loss, and you'll have fun together at the same time. Start with walks and graduate to more strenuous games as he gets fit. Several short sessions of activity a day are just as beneficial as one big effort.

CHAPTER 5

GROOMING
YOUR BOXER

Boxer owners are lucky—your dog's coat needs minimal care. You don't have to worry about coat maintenance issues like daily brushing, shedding, or matted fur. But there is more to dog care than just brushing.

WHY GROOMING IS IMPORTANT

Every dog needs some routine attention to keep him in healthy condition. Weekly exams allow you to find small problems before they become big ones. The Boxer's short coat makes it easier to find nicks, scratches, tumors, fleas, and ticks. As you go over him, look for long, broken, or infected toenails. Check his ears to be sure that they are clean and pink. Look between his toes and on his paw pads for cuts or embedded foxtails. Examine his mouth for excess tartar or inflamed gums.

Grooming should be fun for both of you, not a dreaded chore. It is an opportunity to bond with your dog. Give him a massage or a tummy rub and enjoy your time together.

GROOMING SUPPLIES

The following are basic grooming supplies that you'll need for your Boxer:
- **Gauze:** Use gauze for cleaning the ears and eyes. It can also be used in place of a toothbrush.
- **Grooming glove:** This is a mitten with short rubber bumps on the palm. You will use this item more than any other to groom your Boxer. Use it to remove minor amounts of loose hair or to polish the coat to a glossy finish.
- **Nail clippers:** Guillotine-style clippers have a sharp blade that squeezes shut and trims the nail. Keep extra blades on hand. As an alternative, use a Dremel-style grinder that grinds down the nails instead of cutting them. Pet supply stores carry brands especially made for use on dogs.
- **Rubber currycomb:** A currycomb (like those used on horses) fits in the palm of your hand and has rubber teeth. It brings loose hair to the surface of the coat so that you can brush it away.
- **Shampoo:** For the rare days when your Boxer needs a bath, your choices of dog shampoo are endless. Pick from scented, medicated, all-

PUPPY POINTER

Grooming won't be a problem if you accustom your dog to being touched all over while he is young. Even a young puppy should get tiny toenail trims. Make it a game and use treats to reward him for letting you handle him. Take baby steps and keep sessions short at first.

natural, or other specialty shampoos, depending on your dog's skin condition.

- **Styptic powder:** If you cut a toenail back too far, styptic powder stops the bleeding.
- **Toothbrush:** Specially made doggy toothbrushes usually have a short handle. Or you can use a rubber fingertip brush to massage his gums.
- **Toothpaste:** Don't use toothpaste meant for humans. If a dog swallows some, it can make him seriously ill. Dogs like meat-flavored dog toothpaste, which makes the brushing process easier for you.

COAT AND SKIN CARE

Boxers shed lightly; their coats are so short that their shedding is not as noticeable as in breeds with long hair. The coat sheds more in the spring, mostly over the shoulders and neck. If you see dandruff or your dog's coat feels greasy, something is wrong and you should schedule a visit to your veterinarian. It may be a symptom of a staph infection, allergies, or other skin ailment.

HOW TO BRUSH THE COAT

If he's especially dirty, use the rubber currycomb on his body to lift dirt and loose hair to the surface. Massage your dog's skin in a circular motion to get the best results.

1. Use the grooming glove to brush surface debris and loose hair off the coat.

Dogs like meat-flavored dog toothpaste, which makes the brushing process easier for you.

2. Wipe down his legs and clean between his toes with a damp towel.
3. Clean the face with a damp cloth. Wipe out the folds on his muzzle and under his lips, where moisture and food debris collect.

BATHING

Boxers are naturally clean. Frequent baths aren't necessary if you use the currycomb or grooming glove on a regular basis to remove accumulated dirt, dead skin, and shedding coat. But even the tidiest Boxer can get himself into messes that require the occasional shampoo. Don't bathe your dog too often because it strips the coat of its natural oils. Once or twice a year is probably the most a Boxer ever needs, if that often.

HOW TO BATHE THE COAT

The bathtub is probably the easiest place to bathe your dog. Use lukewarm water because hot water will dry out his skin. Bathing him outside with cold water is fine, although your Boxer may not like it much, especially on a cool day.

To bathe your Boxer:

1. Put cotton balls in his ears to keep water and shampoo out.
2. Soak your dog thoroughly to the skin. A handheld shower massager will push the water into the coat.
3. Add a small amount of shampoo and massage his coat thoroughly. Start with just a teaspoon-sized amount, and add more as you move to other parts of his body.
4. Use a cloth on his face and ears. Take care not to get soap in his eyes.
5. Rinse thoroughly until the water runs clear. Be sure to rinse out all the soap or it could irritate his skin.
6. Let your dog shake off the excess water and rub him down with a towel. Be sure to dry the face

The bathtub is probably the easiest place to bathe your dog.

well so that moisture isn't trapped in the folds of his muzzle. Dry between his toes.

7. Remove the cotton balls and dry his ears, especially if they are uncropped. Drop ears hold moisture and may get infected if not thoroughly dried.

Be forewarned! If you let your dog run loose right after his bath, he'll either rub himself along the walls or roll in the grass outside. Crate him until he is completely dry.

If you feel that you must use a dryer, set it on low so that you don't burn your Boxer's skin through his thin coat.

DENTAL CARE

Just like people, dogs need their teeth brushed regularly. Besides removing excess tartar, the brush massages a dog's gums and prevents inflammation, called gingivitis. As the gums become more inflamed, they recede and pockets form where food and bacteria collect. If left untreated, gingivitis causes tooth loss and infections that can spread throughout the body, causing disease and organ failure. Older Boxers are also susceptible to gingival hyperplasia, a condition caused by inflammation that causes the gums to grow over the teeth.

Boxers have an unusual mouth structure, and this anatomy sometimes leads to increased dental problems. Their deep flews (upper lips) trap food in the mouth, where it causes decay and bad breath.

As you see, tooth care is critically important to your Boxer's overall health. Regular home dental care minimizes the chances that he will experience one of these health problems, and you'll save money on expensive veterinary bills for dental work. Chewing toys and dry food are not enough to keep your dog's teeth and gums healthy. If he has a healthy mouth, brushing at least twice a week should be routine, although daily is ideal. If he suffers from gingivitis, brush daily.

HOW TO BRUSH THE TEETH

There are several types of doggy toothbrushes: a short-handled canine toothbrush and a fingertip toothbrush. Or just wrap your finger with some gauze. Start slowly because your Boxer will initially resist your efforts.

1. Rub his gums gently with your bare finger without trying to pry his mouth open. Then quickly remove your finger and praise him. Add some doggy toothpaste and repeat. He'll soon learn to enjoy the sensation and the taste. Once he's used to it, transition to using the toothbrush.

2. Peel back his lips and brush the teeth and gum line using small circles. Hold the bristles at a slight angle.

3. Next, open his mouth and brush the backs of his teeth using a straight back-and-forth motion. Concentrate on the outside of the molars in the back, where food often gets stuck between teeth and cheek. The dog's tongue does a good job of cleaning the inside (backs) of the teeth.

4. If you can't brush the entire mouth in one sitting, do just a little bit each day until he gets used to it. Reward him with lots of praise and treats.

Without home care, serious gum disease starts in Boxers as young as two years old. Even with regular brushing your dog's teeth will need to be cleaned by a veterinarian at some point, especially when he gets older. But he'll need it less often, will suffer less pain, and will be under anesthesia for a shorter period than if his teeth had had no care. The doctor will scale and polish the teeth and perform a thorough cleaning below the gum line. The vet will also remove any decayed or loose teeth and conduct a complete mouth exam, looking for tumors or other abnormalities.

EAR CARE

If your Boxer has cropped ears you'll easily notice when his ears need cleaning. Once the cropping

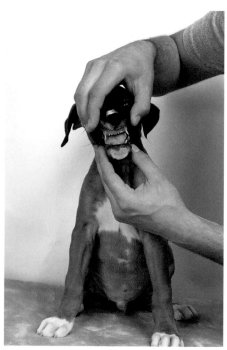

From the time your Boxer is a puppy, regular dental checkups and teeth cleanings are important.

A dog with uncropped ears is more susceptible to ear infections because the ear canal is covered and air doesn't get in as easily.

surgery has healed and his ears are staying upright, cropped ears shouldn't require special care.

A dog with uncropped ears is more susceptible to ear infections because the ear canal is covered and air doesn't get in as easily. Moisture and warmth create the perfect environment for bacteria to flourish and cause infection. Uncropped ears therefore need to be cleaned more often.

Whether they are cropped or not, check your Boxer's ears once a week and clean them only when necessary. Too much cleaning isn't good because some wax is needed to protect the inner ear. Also, don't poke cotton swabs down into the ear. A swab could damage the eardrum or drive foreign objects farther into the ear canal.

Black goop and red inflammation are symptoms of an ear infection or mites. An affected dog will also shake his head and scratch his ears. If your dog is suffering from either, your veterinarian will clean the ears and provide an ointment to apply until the problem clears up. The vet may also provide some ear wash so that you can clean the ears more thoroughly at home.

HOW TO CLEAN THE EARS

1. Use a damp cotton ball or wrap your finger with some gauze. Add a few drops of mineral oil or ear wash if the ears are especially dirty.

2. Wipe the inside of the ear, starting at the inside and wiping outward so that the dirt isn't pushed farther into the ear.
3. Finish up with a dry cotton ball or piece of gauze to remove any remaining moisture.

Check the ears for foxtails in the spring and summer. These nasty little grass seedlings have a sharp point on the end and easily become embedded in the ear. They are difficult to remove once they get stuck. If your dog plays outside in tall grass, check his ears as soon as he comes indoors.

EYE CARE

A Boxer's eyes need very little care. But because the lower lid sometimes sags and Boxers have some facial folds near the eyes, the area must be cleaned regularly to remove any goop buildup.

HOW TO CLEAN THE EYES

1. Wipe out any gunk that gets stuck in the corners of the eyes. Use a piece of damp gauze. (A facial tissue might leave papery residue that irritates the eyes.)
2. If your dog's eyes are runny or red, check to see whether there is a piece of grass stuck under the eyelid.
3. If the irritation persists, take him to the vet. If he has scratched the surface of his eye, he'll need prescription eye drops to ease the pain and help it heal.

NAIL CARE

An active dog who walks and runs on hard surfaces wears down his long toenails, but you should still check them every week for excess growth. Nail growth varies from dog to dog, so you'll soon learn how often your Boxer's need clipping. If you hear his toenails tapping as he walks, it is past

An active dog who walks and runs on hard surfaces will wear down his long toenails, but still check them weekly for excess growth.

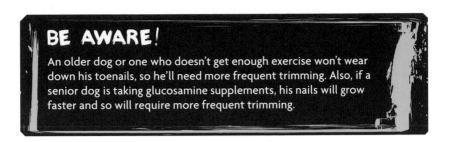

time to trim them. Overly long toenails cause problems because they throw his feet and legs out of alignment. To ease the pain, the dog changes the way he stands and walks. Long toenails also snag and tear, providing an opening for infection to take hold. And to top it off, long nails will mar your hardwood floors and leave nasty scratches on your skin if he jumps on you.

HOW TO TRIM THE NAILS

1. Start with short sessions, less than a minute. Quickly run your hand down his leg and touch his foot. Give him a treat with your other hand and praise him before you let go.
2. Gradually increase the amount of time you touch his foot until he lets you hold it in your hand while he is chewing on a treat. Let go before he tries to snatch his foot away. Make it your idea to stop, not his.
3. Start with just one foot and work up to holding all four feet in turn while praising him and feeding treats. He'll look forward to the attention and offer his foot when you start the "foot game."
4. Tap on his toenails one at a time with the clippers. Praise and treat.
5. Finally, clip a very short bit (less than 1/32nd of an inch [.08 cm]) off the end of one nail. Praise, treat, and let go. Make a vertical cut perpendicular to the foot, not angled.

Work up to where you can do one entire foot, then all four feet in one session.

Your Boxer's dewclaws were probably removed when he was just a few days old. If not, be sure to trim them regularly. The dewclaw is partway up the front leg and doesn't wear down at all. Dewclaws grow in a circle and embed in the dog's leg, causing severe pain and infection.

Using a Grinder

A handheld grinder features an abrasive cylinder that sands down the nail tips. Acclimate your Boxer to the sound and the feel of the grinder the same way you did with the clippers. Because the grinder can get very hot, stop every few seconds to let it cool. Put finger pressure on the nail to cool it and relieve the vibrating sensation.

If You Cut the Quick

The quick is a vein in each nail that grows out to the end, and if the nail is cut too short, the quick bleeds, just as if you cut your own fingernails too short. If your dog has white nails, you can see the quick. But with black nails, assume that the quick is right at the end and cut less.

If you accidentally cut the quick it hurts, and your dog will try to snatch his foot away. Press your finger hard against the end of the nail. Apply pressure for up to five minutes or until the bleeding stops. Apply styptic powder to the end of the toenail to help the blood clot. Let him rest for an hour or so to keep the bleeding from starting again. You may have to do some retraining because your Boxer will be reluctant to get hurt again.

If your dog has really long nails, trim them more often, even every day, so that the quick gradually recedes. Ultimately, the end of each toenail should be even with the end of the toe. It may take several weeks to trim the nails back to this point.

HOW TO FIND A PROFESSIONAL GROOMER

You may wonder why a Boxer would ever need to go to a groomer. Although he rarely needs a bath, you might want professional help if:

• Your Boxer gets skunked or rolls in something really smelly. It's no fun spending

When choosing a grooming shop, consider where your dog will be kept while he is waiting for you to pick him up.

If you can't trim your Boxer's nails yourself, a professional groomer can help.

hours cleaning up the house after you've cleaned up the dog. Groomers use odor-removing shampoos and powerful sprayers that make the job easier.

• You are unable to trim your dog's toenails yourself. Groomers can usually get the job done quickly and easily, especially if they have staff to help.

When choosing a grooming shop, consider these issues:

• Is the shop clean? As the day goes on, there will always be hair and debris around, but does the staff sweep regularly? Do they disinfect or at least clean off the table between dogs?

• Check that dogs are not left unattended on grooming tables. A dog with his neck in a grooming noose could strangle if he jumps off.

• Beware of groomers who leave dogs in a crate with dryers blowing. It quickly gets too hot to be safe. Boxers are especially susceptible to overheating because of their brachycephalic (short) muzzles. A handheld dryer is safer and more effective.

• Is the shop escape-proof? Some groomers leave the front door open on hot days. Could your dog run out the door or jump over a barrier placed in it?

• Do the groomers treat the dogs well? Do they try to make a dog comfortable with his surroundings?

• Where is your dog kept while he is waiting for you to pick him up?

• Do they provide water or walk the dogs if they are there for several hours?

CHAPTER 6

HEALTH OF
YOUR BOXER

L ike any other dog, Boxers are susceptible to contagious diseases, injuries, and inherited disorders. Your Boxer will live a longer, healthier life if you follow a regular schedule of preventive care and checkups.

FINDING A VETERINARIAN

When searching for a new veterinarian, ask for recommendations from your breeder, neighbors, friends, and other Boxer owners. Local kennels, groomers, and obedience trainers also know area vets and can point you in the right direction. Your state's veterinary medical association may have a referral listing, and the American Animal Hospital Association (AAHA) (www.healthypet.com) lists accredited practices on its website.

Schedule a visit and evaluate the staff and veterinarian for yourself. Is the facility clean and well maintained? Are you able to see the vet of your choice? Are the hours convenient? What happens in an after-hours emergency? What is the doctor's background and area of specialty? Is she familiar with Boxer health problems? Does the doctor seem willing to spend time with you and explain things in language you understand?

THE ANNUAL VET VISIT

Once your puppy has had his initial vaccines, he will need an annual wellness exam. This is an opportunity for your veterinarian to:

- **Answer questions:** Now is the time to ask about any concerns you have regarding your dog's health and behavior.
- **Conduct an overall exam:** Dogs are experts at hiding pain and may not show signs of a problem until it is serious. Over the years, your vet will track your Boxer's weight and other indicators so that she can quickly recognize whether there's been a change that indicates illness. The vet will also look for signs of heart disease and other inherited conditions that

When searching for a new vet, ask for recommendations from people you trust.

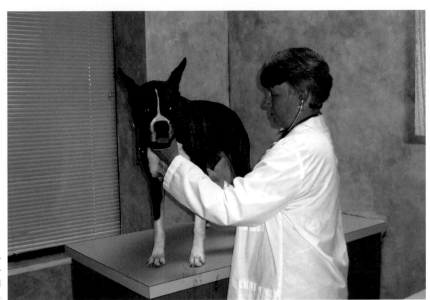

Over the years, your vet will track your Boxer's weight and other indicators.

sometimes affect Boxers.

- **Check for parasites:** The vet will examine a stool sample for evidence of worms.
- **Evaluate dental health:** A thorough mouth exam identifies gum disease, tooth decay, and other abnormalities.
- **Order blood work:** Vets usually require an annual blood test for heartworm and may test thyroid levels and other organ function at the same time.
- **Renew and adjust prescriptions:** If your dog takes regular medication, your vet will review and adjust the dosages.
- **Update vaccines:** Your Boxer should receive booster vaccines every three years. Discuss whether certain diseases are prevalent in your area and whether your doctor recommends any additional vaccines.

VACCINATIONS

A newborn puppy is protected from disease by the antibodies present in his mother's milk. Once he is weaned, he no longer has that protection, so he needs vaccines to protect him as he grows.

Numerous vaccines are available, and there are few absolute answers as to which ones your dog should receive and how often. Your decisions will vary based on where you live, the dog's age, and other risk factors. With that in mind, discuss the options with your veterinarian, and consider the following recommendations.

CORE VACCINES

Most vets agree that there is a short list of core vaccines that are recommended for every dog: distemper, hepatitis, parvovirus, and parainfluenza (DHPP), usually combined in a single injection, as well as rabies. The first DHPP dose, administered when a pup is just six to eight weeks old, primes his system to develop the antibodies he needs to fight disease. Boosters are administered at 9 to 11 weeks, 12 to 14 weeks, and 16 weeks of age. At 16 weeks, the first rabies vaccine is administered. After this series of puppy vaccines, vets recommend a booster at one year.

Your vet will determine which vaccinations your Boxer requires at which stages of his life.

In recent years, scientists have discovered that vaccine protection stays in a dog's system longer than previously believed. After the one-year boosters, the AAHA recommends a booster every three years for the core vaccines.

Because the degree and duration of protection vary based on vaccine manufacturers and from dog to dog, consider having serology testing in place of vaccines. The veterinarian evaluates a blood sample, which indicates whether your Boxer is still adequately protected.

Distemper

An infectious viral disease, distemper starts with upper respiratory symptoms similar to those of kennel cough (refer to "Additional Vaccines" section below) and quickly deteriorates with fever, vomiting, diarrhea, and later, convulsions. Partial paralysis may continue throughout the dog's life. Distemper is transmitted through the air and through direct contact. There is no cure, but treatment of symptoms can keep the dog comfortable until he recovers.

Hepatitis

Infectious canine hepatitis is spread by direct contact with infected dogs.

Hepatitis targets the liver, kidneys, eyes, and blood vessels. Symptoms start with a fever and enlarged tonsils and progress to bleeding and seizures. Veterinarians treat the symptoms to lessen the effects of shock, hemorrhage, and bacterial infections. There is no cure.

Parvovirus

Often fatal, parvo causes bleeding in the intestinal tract. Bloody, strong-smelling diarrhea is the most noticeable symptom, but a dog may also appear to be depressed and in pain. The vet confirms the diagnosis by testing a stool sample. Treatment includes fluids to prevent dehydration and medication to prevent bacterial infections.

Parainfluenza

Highly contagious from dog to dog, this virus quickly spreads through kennels and animal shelters. Symptoms are similar to those of kennel cough, with the addition of sneezing, runny nose, and possible pneumonia. The dog must be quarantined. Parainfluenza is treated with antibiotics, but it often proves fatal.

Rabies

By law, all states require a rabies vaccine. The rabies virus is transmitted in the saliva of infected animals, including wildlife. A dog can show symptoms within a

Bordetella is a highly contagious disease, and the vaccine is usually required before boarding your dog.

week or as long as a year later. Some dogs never exhibit symptoms at all, while others show nervousness that develops into all-out viciousness. The end stages of rabies are gradual paralysis, convulsions, and death. There is no treatment or cure for rabies in dogs or humans, so vaccination is critical.

ADDITIONAL VACCINES

In addition to the core vaccines, there are other vaccines available. Below is a list of vaccines, disease symptoms, and treatments:

Bordetella (Kennel Cough)

Bordetella is highly contagious, and the vaccine is usually required before boarding your dog. Administered either intranasally or by injection, it protects against most upper respiratory infections but not all. Symptoms of the disease are similar to those of a person who gets a cold: coughing, sneezing, and a runny nose and eyes. Treatment includes isolating the dog and giving cough suppressants. In severe cases, a dog can develop pneumonia and require antibiotics. Most dogs recover in one to two weeks.

Coronavirus

Corona is a gastrointestinal virus that causes severe diarrhea and vomiting. Sometimes there are no obvious symptoms. Treatment consists of controlling vomiting and administering fluids to prevent dehydration.

Leptospirosis

A bacterial disease capable of being transmitted to humans, leptospirosis causes fever, vomiting, hemorrhage, kidney, intestinal or liver problems, and pneumonia. Antibiotics and fluid therapy help prevent permanent kidney or liver damage. The vaccine does not always prevent infection, but it does lessen the severity of the disease.

Lyme Disease

Originally identified in humans, Lyme disease is spread by ticks that inject infected saliva when they bite. Symptoms include joint pain and lameness, fever, lethargy, and enlarged lymph nodes. Vets prescribe antibiotic therapy to treat the disease.

PARASITES

Parasites are organisms that feed on their host (a dog in this case) while providing no benefit in return. External parasites live on the body, while internal parasites reside in the heart, digestive tract, or other organs. A heavy infestation of parasites diverts vital nutrients, kills cell tissue, causes anemia, and compromises a dog's immune system, causing serious disease.

EXTERNAL PARASITES

Fleas, mites, and ticks are all common external parasites.

Fleas

These bloodsucking insects multiply rapidly and can transmit tapeworms to their host. You can easily find fleas near the base of your Boxer's tail with a flea comb, or if you turn him over you can see them run for cover on his tummy. Fleas also leave eggs and droppings that look like specks of blood on a dog's skin. Dogs with fleas often develop flea-allergic dermatitis, a condition that causes bacterial infections and thickening of the skin.

Fleas are easily prevented with monthly pills or spot-on preventives that you apply between the shoulder blades. If your home is infested, you must treat the house and yard as well as the dog.

A heavy infestation of parasites diverts vital nutrients, kills cell tissue, causes anemia, and compromises a dog's immune system, causing serious disease.

Check your dog for fleas and ticks after he's been playing outside.

Mites

There are several types of mites that affect dogs: ear mites, demodectic mange mites, and sarcoptic mange mites. Each causes different symptoms and requires different treatment.

Ear mites: If the inside of your dog's ears are brown and goopy or if he tilts or shakes his head and scratches his ears, he may have ear mites. They are contagious to other dogs and cats and also cause bacterial and yeast infections. Easily identified under a microscope, the mites are treated with topical medication.

Other problems can irritate your Boxer's ears, such as allergies or an embedded foxtail, so get an accurate diagnosis from your veterinarian.

Demodectic mange mites: Often seen in Boxers, these mites are transferred from the mother to her puppies. A dog often develops symptoms if his immune system is weakened. Symptoms include hair loss (usually on the face, legs, and feet) and red scaly skin. Demodex usually resolves without treatment once the dog reaches maturity. Vets prescribe miticidal dips in severe cases.

Sarcoptic mange mites: Also called scabies, these mites embed themselves in the skin and cause intense itching. Symptoms include red skin, rash-like bumps, and hair loss, often on the back of the dog's front legs and ears. An infested dog should be isolated and treated with miticidal shampoos and dips. There are also oral medications that kill the mites. Secondary infections are common because the skin is damaged from so much scratching.

Ticks

Another bloodsucking parasite, ticks cause anemia and transmit infectious diseases like Lyme disease and Rocky Mountain spotted fever. Ticks are usually found in tall grass and weeds, especially in open grassy areas during the spring and summer months. Very tiny when it first latches on, a tick engorged with blood looks like a grape hanging off a dog's skin.

Many spot-on flea repellents offer protection from ticks as well. Even so, when you take your Boxer along on hiking and camping trips, check his body and ears, and remove ticks before they attach. Crush the ticks or drop them in alcohol; otherwise they'll just hop right back onto the dog . . . or you.

To remove an embedded tick, use tweezers and grasp the tick at its head against the skin. If you pull just the body, the head will break off and remain embedded. Pull it out without twisting. Clean the area and apply a triple antibiotic ointment or similar first-aid cream.

INTERNAL PARASITES

Internal parasites include heartworms, hookworms, roundworms, tapeworms, and whipworms.

Pick up your Boxer's waste regularly and wash your hands afterward to prevent passing worms to other dogs and family members. An adult dog with chronic worm infestation may not show symptoms.

Heartworms

When a mosquito bites a dog with heartworm, he ingests blood containing heartworm larvae, called microfilariae. The mosquito then injects those microfilariae into the bloodstream of the next dog he bites, where they mature and attack the pulmonary arteries. Symptoms of heartworm infestation include a dry cough and weight loss. As the disease progresses, the dog will lose weight and suffer from congestive heart failure. The treatment is long and harsh. The dog must take an arsenic-based medication for several weeks and be confined to complete crate rest.

PUPPY POINTER

Most puppies are infested with intestinal worms. The first dose of wormer kills adult worms. Your veterinarian will prescribe another treatment in a few weeks to kill worms that were in the larval stage at the time of the first dose.

Heartworm prevention is key. After a diagnostic blood test to ensure that your dog is not affected, your veterinarian will prescribe a monthly heartworm preventive medication. The drug also protects against some other types of worms, so your Boxer gets bonus protection.

Hookworms

About 1/4 to 1/2 inch (.5 to 1.5 cm) long, hookworms attach to the wall of the small intestine and draw blood from the host. Adult dogs come into contact with the larvae in soil or contaminated feces. Unborn puppies can acquire hookworm from their mother. Treat your Boxer with a dewormer from your veterinarian. Heartworm preventives also kill hookworms.

Roundworms

Dogs contract roundworms by coming into contact with the eggs in the soil. If a pregnant bitch has dormant roundworm larvae in her system, the puppies will be infested. Wormy puppies have a dull coat and a rounded, swollen tummy. They may also pass the worms, which look like pieces of spaghetti, in their stool or vomit.

A multi-purpose dewormer will eliminate roundworms in addition to hookworms. Heartworm preventive is also effective.

Dogs contract roundworms by coming in contact with eggs in the soil.

Tapeworms

Fleas eat the eggs of a tapeworm, and when a dog bites at the flea, he ingests the eggs. Tapeworms vary from less than 1 inch (2.5 cm) to several feet (m) long and live in the small intestine. You'll see what appear to be grains of rice in your dog's stool or on his rear end. These are body segments shed by the tapeworm. By controlling fleas on your Boxer, you will also prevent tapeworm infestation.

Your vet will prescribe a cestocidal treatment. Without aggressive flea prevention, tapeworms will quickly reestablish themselves in your dog's system.

Unless you are going to show your dog in conformation, you should alter your Boxer.

Wormers that treat other types of worms are not effective against tapeworms.

Whipworms

The adult whipworm is 2 to 3 inches (5 to 7.5 cm) long and attaches itself to the wall of the large intestine. It is sometimes difficult to detect whipworms in a stool sample. Like other worms, dogs acquire whipworms from contaminated soil or feces. To eliminate whipworms, follow the same deworming program that you used against hookworms and roundworms.

SPAYING AND NEUTERING

Unless you are going to enter him in a dog show, you should alter your Boxer. Pet dogs are usually sold with a spay/neuter contract and a limited registration, meaning any puppies your dog produces will not be able to be registered or shown. A dog with a limited registration can still compete in performance events.

A female dog is altered through spaying surgery, which consists of removing her ovaries and uterus. She will have stitches that need to be removed 10 to 14 days after surgery. Shelter dogs are spayed as early as six weeks, but most owners wait until their pup is six to ten months old but before the first heat cycle, when she is capable of being bred.

A male dog is neutered by removing the testicles to make him sterile. It is a simple surgery unless one or both testicles are retained in the abdomen and haven't descended. Most dogs are up and bouncing around in a few hours. Walk your Boxer on a leash for the next couple of days so that he doesn't rip open his incision. A male can be neutered at any time, but owners usually wait until the age of four to six months.

Besides preventing unwanted litters, there are many other good reasons to alter your dog.

- Altered dogs get along better with other dogs, particularly of the same sex.
- They are less likely to roam and fight, searching for a mate.
- Unspayed females are at risk for mammary cancer or pyometra (an often fatal uterine infection). Unneutered males risk prostate and testicular cancer.
- Raising a litter is expensive. Besides the stud fee, you pay for health screenings, vet visits, worming, puppy vaccines, and litter registration. If the female suffers complications during labor and delivery, she may need a caesarean section to save her and her puppies.
- Responsible breeders guarantee that their puppies are free from genetically inherited diseases. Both parents should be pre-screened for health problems like cardiomyopathy, hypothyroidism, and hip dysplasia. An affected dog should not be bred.
- Only the best of the best dogs should be bred. Do your Boxer's physical characteristics conform to the breed standard? Is his temperament sound, with no hint of aggression or nervousness?

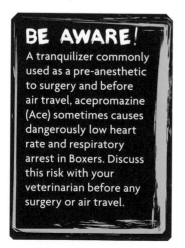

BE AWARE!

A tranquilizer commonly used as a pre-anesthetic to surgery and before air travel, acepromazine (Ace) sometimes causes dangerously low heart rate and respiratory arrest in Boxers. Discuss this risk with your veterinarian before any surgery or air travel.

BREED-SPECIFIC ILLNESSES

The Boxer is a brachycephalic breed, which means that he has a very short muzzle and wide head, compromising his ability to take in air and making him particularly susceptible to heat exhaustion. His unique facial structure also puts him at risk for facial fold dermatitis and allergic reactions to bee stings.

The American Boxer Club (ABC) recommends that breeders test their dogs for the following inherited diseases: aortic stenosis, cardiomyopathy, hip and elbow dysplasia, and hypothyroidism. Some dogs carry the genes and never show symptoms, so testing is crucial. Breeders should provide

White Boxers are especially at risk for skin cancer, so use sunscreen!

puppy buyers with test results certifying that their dogs are free from these conditions. The following list explains these and other issues that occur in Boxers:

AORTIC STENOSIS

An inherited disease in Boxers, aortic stenosis causes the connection between the left ventricle in the heart and the aorta to narrow, restricting blood flow, which causes the left ventricle to work harder. Ultimately the left side of the heart wears out and fails. Dogs may show weakness or even collapse and die while exercising. If your dog is diagnosed with aortic stenosis, medication can treat the symptoms; in extreme cases, surgery is an option.

BLOAT

Deep-chested breeds like Boxers are susceptible to gastric dilation, or bloat, in which the stomach fills with air and in severe cases twists on itself. Bloat blocks food and blood flow and quickly causes death if not treated. Symptoms include restlessness, panting, attempts to vomit, swollen abdomen, dark red gums, and elevated heart rate.

If you think that your Boxer is bloating, take him to the vet immediately. Fluids and relieving the gas may keep his condition from worsening. If the stomach has twisted, he'll require surgery to save his life.

CANCER

Boxers are prone to several cancers. If you find a lump on your dog, have a vet check it out immediately. If caught early, surgical removal may be all that is necessary. White Boxers are especially at risk for skin cancer. Keep your white Boxer out of the sun or use sunscreen and shirts to protect his skin.

CARDIOMYOPATHY

Cardiomyopathy is an electrical abnormality in the heart muscle, also called arrhythmogenic right ventricular cardiomyopathy (ARVC). This form of inherited heart disease is so common that it is identified as "Boxer cardiomyopathy." Affected Boxers can live for years with no symptoms at all, suddenly collapse and die, or gradually show symptoms of congestive heart failure. Researchers have made great strides in identifying carriers of the disease and developing treatment over the past decade, although there is no cure.

If your dog suddenly faints, can't tolerate exercise, or has developed a chronic cough, take him to your veterinarian. Typical indicators like a heart murmur or irregular heartbeat may be hard to identify because symptoms are often intermittent. To diagnose the disease, dogs wear a Holter monitor, which tracks their heart function over a 24-hour period and records any irregular heartbeats. Breeding dogs need to be tested every year, as there may be no signs until the dog is older.

Boxers overheat much faster than breeds with normal facial structure, so provide a cool spot for him to get out of the sun outdoors.

DEGENERATIVE MYELOPATHY (DM)

This neurological disease affects the spinal cord and nerves in the rear end. Most often appearing in middle-aged and senior Boxers, it causes them to gradually develop paralysis and often become incontinent (can't hold their urine and bowels). There is no cure for DM, but some owners buy a cart that supports the dog's hips and back legs so that he can retain some mobility.

GINGIVAL HYPERPLASIA

This is another condition that primarily affects older Boxers. Gingival hyperplasia is excess gum tissue that grows over his teeth. The growths can be removed by surgery, but they tend to come back. Although the cause is unknown, inflammation sometimes contributes to hyperplasia. The best prevention is regular teeth brushing.

HEAT SENSITIVITY

Boxers overheat much faster than breeds with normal facial structure. Limit your dog's exercise in hot or humid weather, provide a cool spot to get out of the sun, and provide plenty of fresh water. Watch for these signs of heatstroke: excessive panting, bright red or too white gums, racing pulse, excessive salivation, or unwillingness to walk.

To treat heat exhaustion, wet your dog's paws, head, abdomen, and chest to lower his body temperature. Take him to the vet even if he appears to recover. Some consequences of heatstroke, such as kidney failure, may not show up immediately.

HIP AND ELBOW DYSPLASIA

Because these are inherited diseases, both sire and dam should be X-rayed before breeding, be declared clear of the diseases, and have a clear pedigree for several generations. The results should be registered with the Orthopedic Foundation for Animals (OFA, www.offa.org) or PennHip (http://research.vet.upenn.edu/pennhip), which grades the hips and elbows from severely dysplastic to excellent.

Dogs affected with hypothyroidism may be lethargic.

In hip dysplasia, the ball and socket of the hip develop abnormally. The ball end of the femur separates from the hip joint, causing pain and arthritis. Hip dysplasia is diagnosed by X-ray when the dog is two years old. While some dogs never show symptoms, surgical hip replacement may be necessary in severe cases.

Elbow dysplasia can be diagnosed by X-ray when the dog is as young as six months. Loose bone chips and arthritic changes in one or both front elbow joints make the dog limp and show signs of pain, especially after exercise. Some cases require surgery to remove the bone chips.

Treatment for both hip and elbow dysplasia includes weight control and moderate exercise like walking or swimming, which help keep the joints flexible and improve the dog's strength.

HISTIOCYTIC ULCERATIVE COLITIS

Boxers less than two years of age are the most susceptible to this form of inflammatory bowel disease, also called "Boxer colitis." Recent research suggests that it is caused by an overactive immune response to bacteria in the colon. Symptoms include mucus and blood in the stool, diarrhea, and the dog's straining to defecate. Treatment includes antibiotics and a high-fiber diet. The condition often disappears on its own as the dog matures.

HYPOTHYROIDISM

A relatively common condition in Boxers, hypothyroidism is caused by a deficiency of thyroid hormone, which regulates the overall metabolism of the body. Affected dogs may be lethargic, gain weight, or have dry, scaly skin. Once diagnosed by a blood test, the condition is treated by administering an inexpensive thyroid pill twice a day for the rest of an affected dog's life, and symptoms should completely disappear.

GENERAL ILLNESSES AND INJURIES

In addition to conditions that specifically affect Boxers, here are some additional health problems that may have an impact on your dog's well-being.

ALLERGIES

Dogs can be allergic to pollen, a specific food ingredient, fleas, mold, grasses, and an assortment of other triggers. Symptoms include itching, runny eyes, ear infections, feet licking, and dry, flaky skin. Secondary infections develop when your dog scratches his skin raw and bacteria enter his system.

Your veterinarian will rule out other causes, such as mites or hypothyroidism, and may refer you to a veterinary dermatologist for further testing. If your dog has an allergy to a particular food, switch to a food that doesn't have that ingredient. It may take several months to see improvement. Many allergies are environmental, and you can't prevent exposure. Sometimes all you can do is treat the symptoms to keep your dog comfortable.

ANTERIOR CRUCIATE LIGAMENT RUPTURE

When Boxers execute their airborne acrobatics, they risk tearing an anterior cruciate ligament (ACL), which is in the rear knee joint. The rupture must be repaired surgically, and the recovery time is 6 to 12 weeks. Dogs who tear one ACL often tear the other one. When you play retrieving games with your dog, throw low and use heavy fetch toys.

ARTHRITIS

A degenerative joint disease usually caused by other diseases like hip and elbow dysplasia, arthritis is common in older Boxers. If your dog ever suffered a torn cruciate ligament or a broken bone,

When Boxers execute their airborne acrobatics, they risk tearing an anterior cruciate ligament (ACL), the rear knee joint.

he is also likely to develop arthritis. Vets prescribe nonsteroidal anti-inflammatory drugs (NSAIDs) for arthritis. Mild exercise such as swimming and supplements like glucosamine and chondroitin keep an arthritic dog's aging joints flexible and improve mobility.

DIARRHEA

Runny stool is a symptom of an underlying problem rather than a disease in itself. Diarrhea can be caused by a diet change, stress, parasites, or something more serious. Prolonged diarrhea causes dehydration. To combat diarrhea, remove regular food and gradually reintroduce a bland diet like boiled chicken and rice. If diarrhea continues for more than 24 hours, see your veterinarian.

RINGWORM

Not actually a worm, ringworm is a contagious fungal disease. It affects the skin, leaving a scaly circular bare patch about 1/2 to 2 inches (1 to 5 cm) in diameter, with red margins around the edge. To diagnose, the vet looks at a skin scraping under a microscope. Mild cases clear up in one to three months, but severe cases require treatment with topical fungicides.

ALTERNATIVE THERAPIES

In recent years alternative therapies have become popular options for treating canine ailments. Often used to complement traditional veterinary care, owners turn to these methods when Western medicine is not working or they prefer to use natural substances to treat their dogs.

ACUPUNCTURE

Based on traditional Chinese medicine, acupuncture is often used to relieve pain, allergies, or arthritis. The Chinese believe that energy, called "chi," flows through the body along pathways called meridians. Needles inserted and manipulated in specific points along these meridians realign the body's natural balance (yin and yang), therefore promoting healing.

CHIROPRACTIC

Chiropractic manipulation addresses problems in the musculoskeletal system. A chiropractor manually adjusts the spine, joints, and soft tissues to relieve pressure and pain. Treatment realigns the spine and also relieves pinched nerves, muscle weakness, and joint pain.

HERBAL

Medicines derived from plants have been used for thousands of years, and animals in the wild are known to instinctively search out herbs when they are sick. Used incorrectly, herbs can cause severe adverse reactions; don't try to formulate your own cures. Some substances may interfere with traditional drugs or cause an adverse reaction, so tell your veterinarian about any you are giving your dog so that their use can safely be integrated into the treatment plan.

HOLISTIC

Emphasizing the use of herbs, homeopathic remedies, and other natural supplements to promote overall health and healing, holistic practitioners approach a problem by looking at the entire animal, including diet, environment, and lifestyle. They focus on preventing illness and maintaining health rather than treating disease once an animal is ill.

Medicines derived from plants have been used for thousands of years.

FIRST AID

Knowing some basic first aid can help save your Boxer's life should he ever become injured. Below are some of the most common medical emergencies.

BEE STING

Because of their facial structure, Boxers are especially vulnerable to insect stings on the face. If stung there by a bee or wasp, your dog's face can quickly swell and block his airway. Take him to the vet immediately.

For less serious stings, scrape the stinger off with a credit card rather than trying to pull it out. If the swelling is not too bad, this home remedy quickly relieves the itching and burning sensation: Mix meat tenderizer with a little water in the palm of your hand to make a paste. Apply to the sting and let dry. Brush off the excess.

BLEEDING

Blood that sprays from a wound may be coming from an artery and cause major blood loss. Slower blood flow indicates bleeding from a vein, which is easier to stop.

A typical Boxer will get some gray on his muzzle and start showing his age at seven or eight.

In either case, apply direct pressure to the wound with a piece of clean material. If that piece becomes saturated with blood, add another one. Don't remove the first; you may dislodge a clot that is forming. You can also apply pressure just above the wound. For serious bleeding, take your Boxer to the vet right away.

If a leg is bleeding, elevate it above the level of the heart. Do not apply a tourniquet to an injured leg. It will do more harm than good, cutting off circulation to the limb.

FOOTPAD WOUND

If your Boxer cuts his paw pad, check for a foreign object such as a thorn or piece of glass. Even a small cut will bleed profusely. Flush out debris with running water. Dry thoroughly, then wrap the paw with gauze and tape it into place. Over the bandage, wrap the foot up to the ankle with an elastic self-stick bandage. Again, don't wrap so tightly that you cut off his circulation. If the cut looks deep, take your Boxer to the vet.

POISON

If your dog has ingested snail bait, a poisonous plant, or other toxin, call the National Animal Poison Control Center for instructions: 888-426-4435. Try to have the package or item in front of you when you call. Don't induce vomiting or give him anything to drink until you have consulted with Poison Control or a veterinarian.

SNAKEBITE

If you live in an area with venomous snakes, consider snake avoidance training for your dog. If he gets bitten, don't try to suck out the venom or use a tourniquet. Keep him quiet to slow the spread of the venom and take him to the vet immediately.

SENIOR DOGS

The average Boxer life span is 10 to 11 years, shorter than for some dogs of similar size but about the same as the larger mastiff breeds from which Boxers are descended. A typical Boxer will get some gray on his muzzle and start showing his age at seven or eight. By taking some steps to ensure his comfort, you'll make his golden years as healthy as they can be:

- Schedule a senior wellness exam. Your vet will do blood work to establish a baseline record so that she can recognize significant changes in his condition.
- An old dog cannot regulate his body temperature efficiently. His short coat and lighter fat layer don't provide the insulation he needs to protect him. Keep him indoors and provide sweaters on cold days.
- Provide a heated or orthopedic bed.
- Older dogs sometimes have trouble walking on slick floors. Put down carpet runners or rugs to help him get around.
- His bladder and bowel control may deteriorate, so take him outside more often.
- As his hearing, vision, and mental faculties decline, he may stand and bark as if he is lost, even in the middle of a familiar room. Have patience when he is confused. Touch him to get his attention if he doesn't respond to you.
- Short walks and swimming will keep his joints flexible.
- Dental care is essential for older dogs. Gum disease and tooth decay can cause organ failure and infections throughout the body.
- Switch to a senior food that is lower in calories but higher in fiber and that uses high-quality meat protein sources. Your Boxer may no longer be able to tolerate fatty table scraps. Senior foods often contain supplements like glucosamine and chondroitin, which ease symptoms of arthritis, help maintain his energy level, and fight disease. Smaller, more frequent meals will stimulate his metabolism and keep him more active. Your dog's appetite may not be what it used to be as his senses diminish; add canned food or moisten his kibble to spark his interest.

TRAINING YOUR
BOXER

Take advantage of the Boxer's innate characteristics when you start training. This breed wants to please and loves an activity that is both mentally and physically stimulating.

Training is a three-step process:

1. Teach the dog what you want him to do.
2. Practice the behavior in a variety of situations until he understands it, performs it reliably with distractions, and makes it a habit.
3. Maintain the behavior by using it in everyday situations and occasional practice sessions.

Because they are so smart, Boxers lose interest if you don't keep them engaged. Repeating an exercise over and over will convince your dog that he hasn't done it right, and he'll invent his own variations. Be patient and keep him focused on you with games, toys, treats, and lots of praise. Once he performs a cue correctly, quit and move on to something else before he gets bored.

Be specific in your commands and demanding in your expectations. Things are pretty black and white in a Boxer brain, so he needs to know that he has to obey—which means that you shouldn't reward him for incorrect behavior. For example: You ask him to sit, but his rear end doesn't quite touch the floor or he bounces right back up. That's his method of trying to get you to do it his way.

WHY TRAIN YOUR BOXER?

Training gives you a language to communicate with your dog and build a relationship. You'll have the tools you need solve problems successfully.

An untrained Boxer is a disaster on four paws, ready to lay waste to everything in his path—and then some. The qualities we love so much in our Boxers are the same ones that make them hard to live with if they aren't trained.

Training gives you a language to communicate with your dog and build a relationship.

Boxers are meant to be housedogs. An untrained Boxer isn't welcome indoors because he won't settle down. He jumps on people, chews the furniture, and guards his territory. Then he gets exiled to the backyard, where he starts digging, barking, and jumping fences. Next stop: animal shelter.

PUPPY POINTER

Young dogs learn quickly but have a short attention span. They can absorb only small bits of information at a time. A 12-week-old dog can easily learn *sit, down,* and how to walk on a leash. In fact, it is often easier to train a puppy than an adult dog because you don't have to break bad habits.

Rescue groups report that Boxers are given up for two common reasons: either the owners didn't understand how much exercise and attention a Boxer needs, or they didn't train the dog and he has become too hard to handle. It's the dog who suffers from our neglect.

POSITIVE TRAINING

Dog training has undergone a revolution in the last 20 years. In the past, instead of focusing on getting the right behavior, instructors concentrated on correcting the wrong one. They spent hours teaching us how to properly yank on the leash to force the dog to comply with our commands. Boxers are sensitive and quit trying if unfairly punished. Verbal or physical corrections don't need to be harsh to be effective.

REWARD

Today's trainers teach us to reward our dogs when they do the right thing. Set your dog up for success and ask for small improvements. Then reward him and quit when he does it so that he remembers that the correct response made good things happen.

Most dogs consider a food treat the best reward on earth. If he likes his regular kibble, you can use that. Other dogs work better for cheese, hot dogs, or semi-moist dog food. Use very small bits so that he doesn't get full and lose interest. Experiment with different rewards—toys, a game, petting—and mix them up to keep training fun and interesting.

It takes up to eight weeks for new behaviors to convert from short-term to long-term memory and become a habit. During this transition, after four to five weeks of training, your Boxer might act as though he's forgotten an exercise he performed just fine yesterday. Take a few steps back and ask for an easier behavior. Once he's successful, work back up to the previous level.

CORRECTIONS

When using positive training methods, how do you correct a Boxer? Sometimes a dog knows exactly what he's supposed to do; he just doesn't want to do it right now. Use the mildest correction possible to get the results you want. If you can't control your Boxer without harsh physical corrections, get help.

Removing your attention is an effective punishment in a dog's eyes. Fold your arms, turn your back on him, and ignore him for a few seconds. Or put him in the crate for a short time-out. You've marked his refusal by ending the fun. He'll remember it. He'll often try again or offer another behavior to win you back.

Don't forget to tell your Boxer when he's done something right. Happy praise and body language communicate better than a gruff "Good dog."

SOCIALIZATION

Socialization means acclimating your Boxer to different people, places, and things so that he is comfortable and willing to try something new. If you properly socialize him, he'll enjoy meeting new people at home and in public. The more positive experiences he has, the better he'll cope with new situations he encounters.

HOW TO SOCIALIZE YOUR BOXER

Socialization is a lifelong project. But if your dog starts young and has positive experiences, he will take new things in stride.

People and Objects

The Boxer is a naturally protective breed, and he needs to know that it's okay for people to come into your home. Introduce him to all kinds of people: children, elderly people, babies, those in

Use very small bits of treats to reward your Boxer so that he doesn't get full and lose interest.

Socialization involves acclimating your Boxer to different people, places, and things.

wheelchairs, and people wearing raincoats and carrying umbrellas. Socialization to objects includes being exposed to things like cars, sprinklers, lawn mowers, dishwashers, fireworks, and marching bands.

Don't force your dog to approach a person or object if he's afraid. How would you feel if a stranger stood over you and shoved a hand in your face? If he appears worried, remove him to a distance where he no longer feels threatened. When your Boxer starts to feel comfortable, allow him to approach at his own speed. Let him explore without anyone trying to pet him, and let him walk away when he's ready.

Your reaction will tell him there is nothing to be afraid of. Encourage him in your happiest voice: "Oh boy, let's go meet some new people!" Don't comfort your dog; he may decide that there really is something to worry about. Or he'll assume that he's being praised for growling.

PUPPY POINTER

A Boxer who goes to his new home at 12 weeks old and never sees another dog will have poor social skills. Enroll in puppy kindergarten as soon as your pup has had his shots. He'll learn his dog manners in a safe and structured environment.

Other Dogs

Controlled play is an important part of a Boxer's education. Without regular exposure to other dogs, he has no experience at reading body language. He'll play too hard and won't know when to quit. Boxers also "box" with their front paws. Because other breeds don't do this, boxing sometimes frightens dogs and causes them to react aggressively.

Set up play dates with friendly dogs. Introduce your Boxer to others at obedience class, the dog park, or the beach. Don't allow unchecked dominance or bullying. Closely supervise his interactions and remove him if he becomes overstimulated (easy for a Boxer). A short time-out may be enough to redirect the play to acceptable levels.

The crate is an essential tool for housetraining, teaching him to hold his urine and bowels.

CRATE TRAINING

Crate training is the act of training your dog to enjoy spending time in his crate. If introduced correctly, a crate is not punishment. Dogs learn to love their crates, and I often find my dogs snoozing away in their crates with the doors open.

WHY CRATE TRAIN?

A home-alone Boxer follows his instincts and guards his property. He reacts to everything he sees or hears, and the resulting anxiety leads to destructive behavior or barking. When crated, he settles down and relaxes because he knows he's not on duty.

There are many good reasons to crate train your Boxer:

- The crate is an essential tool for housetraining, teaching him to hold his urine and bowels.
- A crate-trained dog has a safe place to stay while you have guests.
- A crated dog won't be thrown from a vehicle in an accident and is not as likely to get lost or badly injured.

- When traveling and staying in a hotel, a crated dog can't escape when housekeepers come in to clean.
- When you board your Boxer or he has to stay at the vet's, he'll feel comfortable because he is used to being confined.

It is not fair to crate a dog all day while you are gone and then all night while you sleep. Have someone come in during the day to give your Boxer a break and some exercise.

HOW TO CRATE TRAIN
To crate train your dog:
1. Toss a treat just inside the open crate door. Your Boxer will probably snatch the treat, run off, and eat it across the room. Practice during short sessions throughout the day, using no more than five or ten bits of something yummy.
2. Next, feed him his meals just inside the crate door. Once he's comfortable with that, gradually set the bowl farther back in the crate each time you feed. Pretty soon he'll be running to the crate each time you pick up his bowl.
3. Once he's comfortable with that, close the crate door for just a few seconds. He may be standing with his rear legs out of the crate; a gentle hand on his rump will help guide him inside. Do that once during each meal or treat session.
4. Next, close the door for his full meal, gradually working up to where he stays in the crate for a few extra minutes. Ignore him or rap sharply on the crate if he starts to whine and scratch. Don't reward him with attention. Let him out only when he is quiet and calm.
5. Now, crate him for a few minutes while you sit nearby. Give him a goody to chew on that he normally gets only when he's in the crate. He'll look forward to his time confined. Vary the amount of time he is crated.
6. Gradually work up to where you walk out of the room and return. Don't make a big deal out of it or he'll get anxious as you come and go. Extend the amount of time you are out of the room. By now he should be happy to settle down and relax without a fuss.

HOUSETRAINING
Boxers are relatively easy to housetrain, as they are naturally very clean. Follow a consistent schedule and limit your dog's freedom in the house. He'll quickly learn when and where he should go.

Most adult dogs need to go:
- when they first wake up

Go outside with your Boxer so that you know he has eliminated.

- after breakfast
- midday, after a nap or playtime
- late afternoon or as soon as you get home from work
- after dinner
- before bedtime

Be patient with puppies. They need to eliminate as often as every hour. Once an adult dog is reliably housetrained, he may be able to skip the midday break. If not, have a dog walker or friend come in and let him out.

HOW TO HOUSETRAIN

1. Go out with your Boxer so that you know he has eliminated. Don't play with him or he'll forget the purpose of the outing.
2. Take him to the same spot every time. He'll smell the urine from previous visits and know what to do.
3. If you have other dogs, take them out at the same time. He'll see what they are doing and join the crowd.
4. Reward him with a treat after "mission accomplished."
5. After he's done, give him some free time and attention. When he knows what to expect, he'll get his business done quickly so that he can play, and best of all, come back inside with you.

6. After a potty break, he's earned some free time in the house. After an hour or so, put him back in the crate or take him out again.
7. Pick up his food and water by 8 p.m. It's easier for him to hold it overnight if he doesn't have constant access.

Watch for signs that your Boxer needs to go out, like circling and sniffing, standing by the door, and lining up to aim at a vertical surface (male dogs). Stop him with a loud "No!" and take him outside. If he doesn't go, crate him for an hour and take him out again.

Until he is housetrained, confine your Boxer to the same room with you. If he's been punished for peeing in the house, he may sneak off to another room. Use pet gates between rooms, or close the doors so he won't wander off and get into trouble. When you are not home, leave him in a crate.

ACCIDENTS

If your pup has an accident, don't rub his nose in it or swat him with a newspaper. If you didn't catch him when it happened, he'll have no idea why he's being punished; he'll just learn to be afraid you.

Clean up doggy accidents with an enzymatic stain and odor neutralizer. If any scent remains, he'll go again on the same spot. Soak the area thoroughly with cleaner so that it is absorbed through the carpet and padding, then air-dry.

If your puppy has a housetraining accident, simply clean it with an enzymatic stain and odor neutralizer.

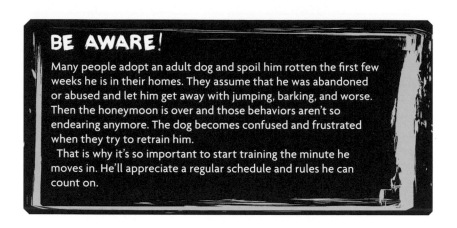

If a previously healthy dog suddenly starts having accidents, there may be a medical reason. Spayed females sometimes develop incontinence and leak small amounts of urine. Inexpensive medication controls this condition. Another possibility is a urinary tract infection. Your veterinarian will need to test a urine sample. Antibiotics usually clear it up quickly.

MARKING

Some so-called accidents are not accidents at all. Both males and females mark their territory with urine, but males seem to be the biggest culprits. If a new dog arrives, supervise both dogs to prevent marking. If it happens, clean the scene of the crime thoroughly and start housetraining over again. Limit your dog's freedom indoors and escort him outside for breaks. A neutered male is less likely to mark. If he has already established the habit, you will need to retrain him after neuter surgery.

BASIC OBEDIENCE EXERCISES

An obedience exercise consists of three steps: 1.) You ask for a behavior; 2.) the dog responds; and 3.) you reward him. Before you teach your Boxer the various commands, pick a release word, like "okay," that tells him he's done. If he doesn't have a clear signal, he'll constantly watch your body language for the slightest clue that he can get up, and it will take a lot longer to train him.

Also, before you start, stock up on some tasty treats. If your Boxer is a food hound and loves everything, use his regular kibble. If he's a fussy eater, cheese bits or hot dog pieces are more likely to get his attention. Chop the reward into tiny bits so that you don't overfeed and he doesn't lose interest. Eventually cut back, eliminating treats completely as he learns to work for praise and attention.

Begin by showing him how to do the exercise. Ask for improvement in tiny increments, for example a 15-second *sit*, then a 30-second *sit*. Anticipate when he's getting ready to make a mistake and release him before he moves. Ending the exercise should be your idea, not his. It usually takes three or four tries before a dog will begin to get the idea and several days to really understand what you are asking him to do.

Once he responds consistently, he must generalize his learning. This means practicing in numerous situations so that your Boxer thoroughly understands. He has a picture in his mind of the *sit* command. At this point it's not just the word that tells him what to do. He pictures you standing in front of him in the living room with a treat in your hand. He doesn't yet understand that "sit" also means sit at the park, the store, or when you're sitting in a chair. By practicing in new places, he'll learn to respond everywhere and be likelier to respond in an emergency.

The *sit* is one of the easiest commands for a dog to learn.

SIT

Sit comes in handy in many situations. Tell your dog to sit when you put on his collar or leash, before he goes out the door, while you groom him, and before you feed. Have him sit to greet friends and strangers, which will prevent him from jumping up on them. Also, the vet can do a more thorough exam if your Boxer is sitting still instead of dishing out kisses!

How to Teach *Sit*

1. With your dog in front of you, hold a treat just above his head. Don't hold it so high that he jumps up.
2. Slowly move it backward so that he has to lean back to see it. He will gradually ease his rear toward the ground. Don't use the word "sit" yet; he has no idea what it means.
3. As soon as his butt hits the

ground, praise him, deliver the treat, and release him.

4. Do this three or four times and he will start to sit as soon as you raise your hand.

5. Once he is sitting reliably, add the *sit* command just as he begins to sit. After several repetitions he will respond to the word and you won't need to lure him.

COME (RECALL)

A reliable *recall* might save your dog's life someday. If he runs off, you want a lightning-fast response before he gets hurt or frightens someone.

When first teaching the *come* command, start with your Boxer on leash and call him from 6 feet (2 m) away.

Your dog should always be thrilled to come to you. If you punish him for coming to you slowly or late, he won't come at all next time. If you have to call him for something unpleasant (like giving medicine), play with him for a few seconds so that he associates coming when called with something more positive. Then move on to whatever you need to do.

How to Teach *Come*

1. Start with your Boxer on leash and call him from 6 feet (2 m) away. Use a happy tone of voice. You'll intimidate him if you stand stiff as a board and issue a strict command. If you have trouble keeping your voice light and fun, say "Come here!" and you'll find that your voice naturally lifts a little.

2. As soon as he looks your way, make a fool of yourself: Jump up and down, praise him to the skies, and tell him what a great dog he is. He'll come bounding in to romp with you in no time. Encourage him the entire way. (Once he knows the command you can calm down a little, but always make returning to you a fabulous thing.)

3. Gradually add distance and distractions to really cement the command in his brain. Switch from the leash to a long line so that you'll still have control when he is farther away. Let him get distracted and practice calling him. Only call once or he will decide that "come, come, COME!" is the command, and he'll wait for the third or fourth call. If he ignores you, gently reel him all the way in if you have to. If he ever gets away with refusing, he'll be much less reliable.

4. Praise him and play for a few seconds before you release him, and try again. As always with Boxers, after a few repetitions he'll start working on creative ways to change the game. Keep it interesting by tossing a ball or toy when he gets to you.

To help your dog become really reliable, play *recall* games with your family and friends. One by one, call your dog. As he runs toward you, encourage him enthusiastically while everyone else remains silent.

How do you get a reluctant dog to come to you? Here are some tips:

• Make yourself more interesting than whatever he is doing; toss a ball or tease him with a toy.

• Crouch down and open your arms wide. Smile and laugh.

• Lie flat on the ground. He'll run up and start sniffing, trying to figure out what's going on.

• Run away from him. He's very likely to chase you.

STAY

Wouldn't it be nice to chat with a friend while your dog sits patiently at your side? The *stay* teaches him to settle down, be patient, and mind his manners in a variety of situations, all vital Boxer skills.

The *stay* teaches your Boxer to settle down, be patient, and mind his manners in a variety of situations.

How to Teach *Stay*

1. As soon as he understands the *sit*, vary the length of time he must sit. Practice releasing him at various intervals—like 15 seconds, then 30, then 10, then 45—so that it's not predictable.
2. As he starts to get the idea, add the *stay* command and hand signal, which is your open palm in front of his face.
3. Release him just before he breaks the *stay*. Go back and touch him so that there's no question when it's okay to get up. When he goofs, and he will because it is part of the learning process, he'll start to get restless and think about standing up. Stop him with a "No!" to get his attention. He'll settle back into the *sit*. If he gets up, just put him back without a word. Take him all the way back to where he originally started, or he'll learn to creep forward. This will escalate to all kinds of Boxer games like rolling around, pawing the air, and other attempts to distract you.

Practice the *stay* at random distances and lengths of time. When you lengthen the time, shorten the distance and vice versa. Then add distractions like bouncing balls or kids running by. Stand closer to him until he understands. Practice while you prepare his dinner or watch TV. Incorporate short *stays* into his daily walks.

DOWN

The *down* is a submissive position, and some dogs don't like to yield their status in the household. Physically shaping a Boxer into position usually starts wiggly-kissy games, so stock up on some patience when you start teaching the *down*. Staying calm will make your efforts more successful. Sometimes a short exercise session first will take the edge off so that he settles down and listens.

How to Teach *Down*

1. Put your Boxer into a *sit* and hold a treat on the ground between his feet.
2. Slowly move the treat away, encouraging him to lower his elbows down on the ground.
3. Once his front elbows touch the ground, praise, give a treat, and release him. Reward him while he is in the correct position.
4. After a few tries, pull the treat farther until he lowers his rear end. Pause a second, treat, and release him.
5. Once he is offering the *down* reliably, add the verbal command and gradually use less of your body language to cue him. Your ultimate goal is to have him do a *down* on command while you are standing straight up.

Another method for teaching a puppy also works with some adult dogs: Lure him with a treat under your bent knee while you sit on the ground.

Expect precision from your Boxer. He will test you and try not to go completely down, using all kinds of creative maneuvers: Elbows down, butt up; elbows a few inches (cm) off the ground; roll over on his back; etc. Don't play by "Boxer rules." Be patient and make your criteria perfectly clear: no treat until he does a real *down*.

I like to play an obedience game that I call "sit-ups." I ask for a *down* and then a *sit* for several repetitions. As he pops up and down he's learning to listen and have some fun, and the game also speeds up his responses. Boxers love mental as well as physical exercise, and training games keep them interested.

HEEL (WALK NICELY ON LEASH)

A dog who drags you down the street is no fun to take for a walk. *Heel* position means that the dog's right ear is lined up with your left leg, without him pulling ahead or lagging behind. He should be able to hold this position while walking on a loose leash.

How to Teach *Heel*

Start in the backyard and let your dog drag his leash:

1. Start walking and talk to him, jump around, wave your arms, slap your leg, or hold a toy or treat. Make yourself more interesting than all the other exciting things around him.
2. Whenever he looks your way or joins you, praise and reward him with a treat.
3. Do short (one-minute) sessions at first. Soon he'll be happily following you around the yard. Every time you stop, ask him to sit.
4. When his attention wanders, turn suddenly or dash off in the opposite

direction so that he thinks he missed something exciting. Praise him when he rejoins you.

5. Stop occasionally and give him a jackpot: an entire handful of goodies. He doesn't know when to expect another jackpot, so he'll be very attentive.

Now repeat this routine while holding the leash:

1. Once you pick up the leash, don't get lazy. Keep his interest and include frequent *sits*, *downs*, *stays*, and rewards in his walking routine.
2. When your Boxer starts to pull, stop and stand perfectly still. You are not going to move until you have his attention and he sits.
3. When you start walking again, expect him to lunge to the end of the leash. Be ready to stop and start over. After a few one-step walks, he'll anticipate and remain calm when you start forward again.
4. Gradually work up to two steps and then three or four before you stop and have him sit. If he starts pulling again, go back to one step at a time.

You want your dog to be able to walk on a loose leash while he sniffs and explores. If he constantly has to focus on you, it's a lot of work and tiring for both of you. As he learns his leash manners, give him more freedom. Continue to praise and reward him for not pulling.

FINDING A PROFESSIONAL TRAINER

Everyone benefits from obedience classes, even if you have raised a dog before. A good instructor helps you sharpen your skills while working through training and problem behaviors. Classes are also an excellent place for supervised socialization.

WHERE TO FIND RECOMMENDATIONS

So how do you find the best instructor for you and your Boxer? Ask for recommendations from:

• other Boxer owners or your breeder
• your veterinarian
• local obedience clubs or the humane society
• parks and recreation department in your city
• national associations: Association of Pet Dog Trainers (APDT, www.apdt. com), International Association of Canine Professionals (IACP, http:// canineprofessionals.com/Public/FindAProfessional.aspx), National Association of Dog Obedience Instructors (NADOI, www.nadoi.org)

HOW TO PICK THE RIGHT INSTRUCTOR

Dog trainers are not required to have any type of certification. But membership in

Obedience classes can help your Boxer become a better-behaved member of the family.

professional organizations like the APDT or a local obedience club tells you that a trainer keeps up on the latest trends and methods.

- **Ask about the trainer's experience with Boxers.** Some misunderstand Boxers, thinking they are stubborn or impossible to train. How long has the trainer been teaching? Where did she learn? How does the instructor deal with small and large dogs in classes together? What equipment does she recommend?
- **Ask whether you may observe a class.** Are the students having fun? Are they successful? Do you like the instructor's methods? What is the ratio of instructors and assistants to students? Is each student getting personal attention? Do students get answers to their questions?
- **Ask about the extras.** Are advanced obedience or fun classes available after you complete the first class? Does the instructor offer private lessons if you need extra help?

CHAPTER 8

SOLVING PROBLEMS
WITH YOUR
BOXER

Barking, chewing, digging—these are natural ways that dogs express themselves and occupy their time. But when these activities don't fit into our lives, they are labeled problem behaviors.

Deal with issues before they become habits or it will take much longer to retrain your pet. Here are some general tips to prevent trouble:

- **Management:** Control your dog and his environment to prevent trouble before it happens. Block his view so that he's not encouraged to bark and guard his territory. Crate him when you can't supervise his behavior. Put him on a leash so that you can control his actions, even around the house.

- **Mental exercise:** Boxers are intelligent problem solvers and need a job to keep their minds busy. When all that excess mental energy isn't channeled, they create their own entertainment. Puzzle games, hide-and-seek, or other thinking games are excellent ways to occupy your dog.

- **Physical exercise:** Training and vigorous exercise are an important part of any Boxer's daily routine. A quick walk around the block every evening is not enough to meet his needs. Monks of New Skete dog trainer Job Michael Evans once wrote: "A tired dog is a good dog." This certainly is the case for Boxers. Most Boxer problem behaviors can be attributed to their tremendous amount of energy; if not channeled appropriately, it results in a long list of unwanted behaviors. If you can't provide enough exercise, take your Boxer to doggy day

Training and vigorous exercise are an important part of any Boxer's daily routine.

care or hire a dog walker.

- **Schedule:** A dog is less anxious and likely to act out if he has a daily routine he can count on. Feed him, come home, go for walks, put him to bed, and engage in other activities at about the same times and he'll soon relax, confident in

what the day will bring. If your dog has issues, hire a pet sitter to come in and give him attention when you can't get home on time.

- **Time with you:** Boxers are not meant to spend their days alone, isolated from their families. The more time your dog gets to be with you, the better he'll behave. Even sleeping in a crate next to your bed is time with his "pack," which is comforting to him.
- **Training:** Basic obedience—including commands like *sit*, *down*, and *stay*—teaches a Boxer self-control. After a few weeks of classes and practice, he'll start to settle down as he learns the rules and knows what is expected of him. He'll be more confident with some structure in his life. Many problems resolve themselves without further intervention.

AGGRESSION AND GUARDING BEHAVIOR

Historically, Boxers were used for bear and bull baiting, and for a short time, fighting. They needed a bold and assertive temperament to stand up to their foes. Today's Boxers retain these characteristics. While not naturally aggressive, Boxers do need training and leadership to keep their dominant traits under control.

WHY DOGS ARE AGGRESSIVE

Aggression is triggered by stress and/or fear, usually caused by a buildup of several events at once. It sometimes develops as the dog reaches full maturity, when he's about two years old. Learn to read your dog's body language and recognize when he is uncomfortable.

Most aggression toward humans is really territorial guarding behavior. But once the person is welcomed into the owner's home, that stranger instantly transforms into the dog's best buddy.

Most aggression toward humans is really territorial guarding behavior.

HOW TO PREVENT AGGRESSION

- **Protect your Boxer.** He should never feel that he has to defend himself from a person or dog. When you realize that he is stressed, remove him before the situation escalates.
- **Train your Boxer.** Basic obedience training gives you the tools to control your dog. He'll then look to you for leadership and won't be as likely to assume that job for himself.
- **Socialize your Boxer.** Start from the minute he arrives in your home. Teach him that people and dogs coming to the house are friends. Take him out in public to meet people and animals so that he is used to meeting friendly strangers.
- **Alter your Boxer.** Have the surgery performed before he is one year old. Any dogs can develop a rivalry, but unaltered dogs of either sex are the most likely to quarrel.

HOW TO MANAGE AGGRESSION

Aggression of any kind is not something to take lightly. If your dog's behavior seems aggressive:
- Take him to the vet to get a full physical checkup.
- Seek professional behavioral help before it becomes a serious problem.

BARKING

Excessive barking isn't just irritating. It annoys your neighbors and frightens people who come to your home. You'll have more problems than just a barking dog if you don't get it under control.

WHY DOGS BARK

There are many reasons why dogs bark. The Boxer is a guard dog with ultra-sensitive hearing. He notices everything and everyone that comes near his territory. This behavior is often unintentionally reinforced because the person he's barking at—for example the mail carrier—goes away.

Picture the mail carrier from your Boxer's point of view. Every day, this stranger wearing a uniform and a big hat (two things many dogs are afraid of) comes to the front door wielding a large bag of who knows what. As soon as Boomer barks, the mail carrier leaves. Success! Boomer's chased him away! And it works every day, reinforcing the dog's barking and guarding instincts.

A few successes like that and the next thing you know, you have a recreational barker who spends his time looking for an excuse to sound the alarm. It won't take much to get him started: a bird flying overhead, a car driving by, a ringing phone, or the next-door neighbor clearing her throat within earshot.

HOW TO MANAGE BARKING

There are a few effective ways to manage excessive barking:
• Interrupt your dog's barking and redirect his behavior to an acceptable activity. If you don't give him something else to do, he'll just start barking again. When you yell at him he figures that you're just barking along with him. Additionally, in his mind, negative attention is better than no attention at all. Go get him, snap

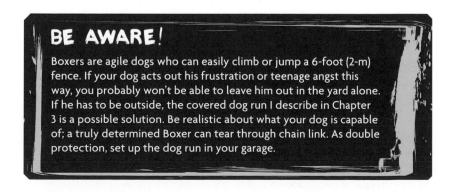

BE AWARE!

Boxers are agile dogs who can easily climb or jump a 6-foot (2-m) fence. If your dog acts out his frustration or teenage angst this way, you probably won't be able to leave him out in the yard alone. If he has to be outside, the covered dog run I describe in Chapter 3 is a possible solution. Be realistic about what your dog is capable of; a truly determined Boxer can tear through chain link. As double protection, set up the dog run in your garage.

on a leash, and walk him inside for a short time-out. When you let him back out, attach a long line so that you can control him. If he starts barking again, reel him in with the line. Reward him when he quits and comes to you. If nothing works, put him into his crate and don't let him out until he is quiet. Cover the crate with a blanket if you have to.

Sufficient exercise can help prevent a lot of problem behaviors.

- Your dog may be so focused on barking that you can't get his attention. To interrupt him, toss a can of pennies or bang two metal dishes together to startle him. As soon as he looks in your direction, praise and call him away from the source.

- Block his view. Close the drapes or keep him out of the living room if he barks at passersby. Outdoors, build a solid fence or plant a hedge so that he can't see the neighbors.

- Teach him to bark on command. I know it sounds like the exact opposite of what you want, but you are creating an "off" switch. Teach him to speak and reward him when he barks. When you see him getting ready to stop, use your command: "quiet," "no bark," or whatever word or phrase you choose. He'll eventually associate the word with quiet. Reward him when he stops, even if just for a few seconds.

CHEWING

Chewing is a totally natural and necessary behavior. A dog needs to chew to maintain the health of his teeth, jaws, and gums. Every Boxer owner I talked to for this book told terrifying tales of canine destruction. One owner described how her Boxer shredded a down comforter and she was still finding feathers six years later. Other Boxer chewing expeditions included fencing, couches, door molding, shoes (designer labels appear to taste better), dog beds, clothing, Christmas trees, and trash cans.

WHY DOGS CHEW

Dogs chew for a variety of reasons. Puppies use their mouths to explore the world; they don't have hands like human babies, so they taste everything. Teenage dogs are getting their adult teeth and their gums ache, so chewing relieves inflammation and pain. If allowed to become a habit, long after your dog's finished teething he'll still enjoy chewing.

HOW TO MANAGE CHEWING

You can prevent problem chewing in the following ways:

- Limit your Boxer's access to chewables. Crate him in a sturdy escape-proof crate when you're not home. If you lock him in the bathroom, you're likely to return to a pile of shredded towels and an uprooted toilet. He's safer where he can't get to anything.
- Give him several frozen chew toys. Frozen treat-filled toys are great because they last for a while. Ice cubes are also an excellent option. In the summertime I fill a plastic bowl with water and an assortment of treats: spoonfuls of peanut butter, kibble, biscuits, apples, carrots, zucchini, and leftover chicken. I freeze it and then dump it out into a dish. It keeps my dogs busy for several hours as it melts and gives up its treasures. You can even try a frozen washcloth; just like a human pacifier, a frozen washcloth helps soothe the sore gums of a dog who is teething.
- Shut doors or use pet gates to keep him out of rooms when you can't watch him.
- Install childproof locks on cabinet and closet doors.
- Put trash cans out of reach.
- Spray objects with bitter apple spray so that the bad taste deters him. (Be careful not to stain your furniture; pre-test repellents on a hidden spot.)

If you catch your dog chewing, correct and redirect him. Take away the object, bribing him with a treat if you have to. Then offer something he's allowed to chew as an alternative.

Supervise your dog's toys and take them away when they start to fall apart.

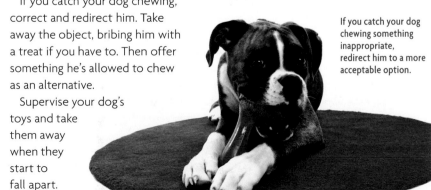

If you catch your dog chewing something inappropriate, redirect him to a more acceptable option.

Dog Tale

My friend Cindy Jobs told me this story about her Boxer Harley:
"We keep an extra refrigerator in the dog room. One morning my husband Roger was getting something out of it and Harley was standing in the doorway with an "Oh, that's how that works" look on his face. When we got home that evening, he'd opened the fridge and emptied it. The damage included three bottles of salad dressing (he'd chewed the tops, so there was oily salad dressing everywhere), six romaine hearts (now shredded), and six beers (with holes punched in them so beer sprayed everywhere).

"Until we could get a Harley-proof refrigerator, we just taped it shut. When we had the new refrigerator delivered we asked them to leave the handles off. We haven't had any issues since."

DIGGING

Boxers usually need a reason to dig, and their excuses are many.

WHY DOGS DIG

If your dog isn't neutered, he can sense a female in heat from several miles (km) away, and unspayed females also frantically try to escape when they're in heat. Boredom and lack of exercise, the causes of most Boxer problem behaviors, also contribute to digging. A lonely dog left in the yard all day digs, sometimes to escape and sometimes just for something to do. Gophers, moles, and ground squirrels also motivate dogs to excavate the yard. And in hot weather, dogs often dig out a cool spot under a bush or against the house.

HOW TO MANAGE DIGGING

The following are some suggestions to thwart your digger:
- If your dog is digging because he's seeking out critters in the dirt, the obvious solution is to get rid of the pests, but be careful what measures you use. If your dog eats a poisoned rodent, he could get sick and die. Rid your yard of unwelcome critters by using humane traps, which are effective and much safer for household pets.
- If your dog is digging because he's hot, buy a raised mesh dog bed, which allows air to circulate around his body. Place one in his favorite resting spot. Also, fill a kiddie pool with water so that he has a place to cool off.

- If you have a garden, put your Boxer indoors while you are digging. Spray your plants and the surrounding soil with animal repellent. Bury wire mesh or large rocks around the base of new plants.
- Put water balloons in the holes and fill the holes with soil. When he digs there again, the balloons will pop and scare him. This is called an environmental correction. That hole punished him—you didn't.
- Bury his feces in the hole. The unpleasant smell will often be enough to stop him.
- Make a digging pit for your Boxer. Fill it with soft soil or sand, and bury smelly treats or toys. Praise him when he digs in that spot. Don't give up; it may take a week or more for him to get the idea.
- Bury chicken wire or hardware cloth along the bottom perimeter of your fence. Staple it to the wood and then run it into the ground for a few inches (cm). Cover with soil or gravel. The unpleasant sensation of snagging his toenails on the wire and rocks will stop him. Also bury wire mesh in holes he has dug in the yard.
- For the dedicated escape artist, pour a cement curb around the base of your fence.
- The final solution, if nothing else works, is to keep your Boxer indoors in a crate when you can't supervise him.

In hot weather, dogs often dig out a cool spot under a bush.

HOUSE SOILING

Boxers don't usually forget their housetraining, so if yours does, there is probably something else behind it.

WHY DOGS HOUSE SOIL

First suspect a medical problem. If your dog urinates inside, he might have a urinary tract infection. Females sometimes suffer from incontinence (meaning they leak urine), which is manageable with medication. Watch to see whether your dog is licking herself; her skin may be irritated from being constantly moist. If your dog defecates inside, collect a sample and take it to the vet for analysis, especially if the stool is runny or you see blood or mucus. He may have a parasite or other digestive irritation.

Once you rule out medical problems, there are other reasons a Boxer may have an accident:

- Does he get outside often enough? Are you sure he relieves himself before he goes to bed at night?
- Are you missing the cue that he needs to go outside? Circling and sniffing are sure signs that he needs to go.
- Did you change his potty area? Is there gravel where there used to be dirt? Did you remove his favorite pee bush? He may be confused about where he is supposed to go.

Make sure that your Boxer puppy is getting outside to eliminate often enough.

Dog Tale

Cindy came home on a Friday from a long week at work. She opened the door to the dog room and found that her Boxer, Harley, had opened all five of the drawers and one cabinet. He'd emptied the first 6 inches (15 cm) of all the drawers and most of the contents of the cupboard. There were nuts, bolts, screws, tape measures—an assortment of home improvement products—strewn across the floor. In addition, he'd pulled out the electric griddle (which must have smelled like bacon) and chewed the plastic parts. Poor Annie (also a Boxer) had stepped in some putty and had screws and cup hooks stuck to her paws. On Saturday, Cindy installed child safety locks on all the doors and drawers.

- Has there been a change in the daily routine at your house? Have you moved? Has someone moved in or out? Have you started working when you used to be at home all day? Have you had company staying with you? Is there a new pet? These kinds of things upset his routine and may cause him to make a mistake.
- Other stresses also contribute to a dog's confusion. If there is tension between family members, dogs sense it and, just like children, act out their worries.
- Is it rainy or snowing outside? He may just be a prima donna and not want to get his feet wet!
- Is he marking his territory? Although this usually involves males, females mark too.

HOW TO MANAGE HOUSE SOILING

No matter what the reason is for this turn of events, handle it the same way. Start over with his housetraining:
- Keep a consistent schedule of meals and breaks; give him limited freedom in between.
- Catch him in the act and take him outdoors.
- Go out with him and praise him when he eliminates.
- Pick up his water at least an hour before his last potty break of the night.
- Don't let him out of your sight. Confine him to the same room you are in. Tie him to your chair if you have to.
- Crate him when you can't supervise.

JUMPING UP

An excited Boxer will sometimes charge up and body slam you, hitting your chest with his front paws. If you didn't teach him not to jump on you when he was a puppy, now is the time!

WHY DOGS JUMP UP

Your dog may have good intentions when he jumps up—he wants to greet you and smell your breath the way a submissive puppy would. But jumping up is downright dangerous. Boxers are so boisterous that even a less overwhelming greeting can injure a person. Also, Boxer greetings usually include big wet kisses, a real turnoff if your guests aren't dog lovers.

Boxers are so boisterous that even a less overwhelming greeting can injure a person.

HOW TO MANAGE JUMPING UP

- Teaching a dog not to do something is more abstract than asking him to perform a specific command. With that in mind, teach your Boxer to sit when he greets someone. If he is sitting, he can't jump or otherwise misbehave. To teach this, attach a leash and have a volunteer helper approach you. Ask your dog to sit. If he doesn't comply, walk him away and try again. Have him sit when the person is still a short distance away, when it is easier for him to control himself. Reward him with praise and a treat, and continue practicing until he sits with the person right in front of him. He won't be perfect the first day or even the first week, but he'll eventually get the idea. With an exuberant, people-loving breed like a Boxer, it may take longer to learn.
- If you want him to jump on you for a hug or greeting, teach him to jump up by invitation. Pat your chest and use a command like "up" or "hug." Also teach your Boxer "off" by saying it as he bounces back to the ground. I recommend the word "off" as opposed to "down" because we've already taught him that "down" means "lie down." "Off" means "four-paws-on-the-floor and no exceptions."

- When he jumps on you and you push him off with your hands, you've just rewarded him. He'd love to start wrestling. Fold your arms and turn away, denying him any attention. Wait until he drops back to the floor and praise him quietly. This may take a few minutes, but the time will shorten as he learns. He'll probably jump right up again as soon as you make eye contact. Repeat the sequence until he stays off.
- Let him drag a leash in the house, and when he starts to jump up, step on it. He'll self-correct, stopping mid-leap. Attach a long line when he's outside so that you can enforce the *off* command if he jumps on someone else.
- If he's out of control when company comes, confine him to his crate for a short time. Bring him out on a leash and try again until he greets people without jumping. Return him to the crate as many times as you need to.
- When you first arrive home, don't greet him immediately. He's probably been napping and needs to relieve himself anyway. Take off your coat, change clothes, and get a drink before you calmly greet him as though it's no big deal. He'll learn that there's no reason to go crazy when you arrive.

NIPPING

Nipping, or play biting, starts when a Boxer is a puppy.

WHY DOGS NIP

As I mentioned before, puppies explore the world with their mouths. They also use their mouths to play with their littermates, biting and roughhousing. When a puppy nips his sibling too hard, the offended pup yips and leaves, thus ending the game. The biter learns not to use his teeth so hard next time. This early play starts teaching him doggy manners. It's up to you to continue his education when he comes to live with you.

HOW TO MANAGE NIPPING

No dog should ever be allowed to put his mouth on you. If your pup is now an adult and has not learned this essential bite inhibition, start teaching him the same way you would train a puppy.
- Use dog body language. When he nips, yelp loudly, turn away, fold your arms, and leave. Ignore him for a few minutes to impress upon him that you did NOT like being bitten. Pretty soon he'll get the point. If you push him away, he'll think that you are playing and will nip even more. Even children can discipline a puppy in this manner. Kids tend to wave their arms and run around, which unintentionally encourages him to nip.

- If a puppy or adult dog gets too excited, put him in a time-out for a while. This will give everyone a chance to calm down.

FINDING A PROFESSIONAL BEHAVIORIST

We aren't born knowing how to train dogs, any more than we know how to train elephants. Don't be shy about seeking out a professional to help you with behavior issues.

WHEN TO SEEK HELP

Seek a professional behaviorist if any of the following describe you or your Boxer:

If your Boxer is now an adult and has not learned essential bite inhibition, start teaching him like you would train a puppy.

- Your dog has snapped or growled at anyone, at home or in public.
- Your Boxer is overly territorial.
- Your dog guards his toys or food or growls when asked to get off the furniture or move out of your way.
- Your dog is just too much to handle: too excited, too rowdy, too hard to walk.
- You have tried to solve a problem yourself and have been unsuccessful.
- You are afraid of your dog.

HOW TO FIND A BEHAVIORIST

Start your search by talking to your obedience instructor. Your trainer may have experience teaching classes but may not be qualified to deal with aggression or other major behavior issues. Ask the trainer to refer you to a more qualified expert.

A qualified consultant identifies and helps you work through your dog's specific issues. There are several types of dog behavior consultants, and each has an increasing level of education and experience. Specific organizations train and certify these experts, and many have a database of people you can contact for help.

International Association of Animal Behavior Consultants (IAABC)

The IAABC (www.iaabc.org) requires members to demonstrate competency in six core areas of behavioral science and counseling. The IAABC also endorses using the least aversive methods possible to achieve the desired results.

BE AWARE!
Keep a leash and treats in strategic places—like at the front door, in the car, and in your coat pocket. Hook him up when you need to get an exuberant Boxer under control quickly.

Animal Behavior Society (ABS)

The ABS (www.animalbehaviorsociety.org) certifies applied animal behaviorists. Members must achieve a graduate-level degree in animal behavior and must also study learning theory, zoology, comparative psychology, and other disciplines. They also must have three to five years of professional experience.

American College of Veterinary Behaviorists (ACVB)

Most veterinarians do not have enough in-depth training and experience in animal behavior to address serious problems. Ask your veterinarian for a referral to a veterinary behaviorist. These professionals are certified as Diplomates of the American College of Veterinary Behavior (www.dacvb.org). They have completed a two-year residency under the guidance of a board-certified veterinarian and are licensed to treat both medical and behavioral issues. Unlike other types of consultants, veterinary behaviorists can prescribe medications to treat your Boxer's issues.

Other Organizations

Several additional organizations offer certification in behavior counseling, and their websites list professionals qualified to assist you: the Association of Animal Behavior Professionals (AABP, www.associationofanimalbehaviorprofessionals.com) and the Association of Companion Animal Behavior Counselors (ACABC, www.animalbehaviorcounselors.org).

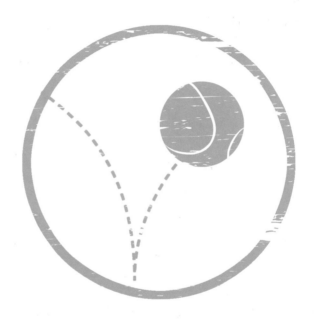

ACTIVITIES WITH YOUR BOXER

There is a wide variety of activities for Boxer lovers, both competitive and noncompetitive. Boxers excel in traditional dog sports, like obedience and Schutzhund, and newer activities, like herding, where they have only recently begun to showcase their talents. The American Kennel Club (AKC) sponsors many of the activities profiled here. The United Kennel Club (UKC) and other activity-specific organizations also offer canine sports.

COMPETITIVE DOG SPORTS

If you aren't fiercely competitive, there are still plenty of awards within your reach. And you don't even have to win first place to earn titles. In most competitions, you perform certain exercises and must earn a minimum number of points to qualify. After a specified number of qualifying entries, you earn the title.

Your dog does not have to be an AKC-registered Boxer to compete in competitive sports. The AKC offers the PAL (Purebred Alternative Listing, formerly called Indefinite Listing Privilege, or ILP). With the PAL, your dog is eligible for all performance events except conformation. PAL dogs are required to be spayed or neutered. If you purchased your Boxer with an AKC limited registration, meaning he can't be bred, he doesn't need a PAL.

Navigating tire jumps are just one of the many activities that agility offers.

Conformation evaluates a dog against the standard for the breed.

AGILITY

Agility is the perfect sport for an active Boxer. The action is fast but precise, challenges an intelligent breed like ours, and is an exciting way to have fun with your dog. While remaining under the handler's control, each dog is required to complete an obstacle course within a specified time limit without committing any faults. Challenges include climbing over an A-frame, walking across a teeter-totter, running through a tunnel, and jumping through tires. There are several organizations in the United States that offer agility events, and each has slightly different requirements. Check out the United States Dog Agility Association (USDAA, www.usdaa.com) and the North American Dog Agility Council (NADAC, www.nadac.com).

CONFORMATION

Originally held to evaluate potential breeding stock, dog shows have become a popular sport over the past century. The Westminster Kennel Club dog show is an example of a conformation event. Judges evaluate how well a dog conforms to the established standard for his breed. Dogs must have registration papers and be intact (not spayed or neutered). Classes are separated within the breed by age, sex, and other factors. The winners in each class move up to the Best of Breed judging. The winning Boxer then competes in the Working Group against other

Dog Tale

My friend Dena tells me that her Boxer Maddux has made her a better trainer. She has to constantly analyze her training and try new methods because the dog is usually one step ahead of her. At one obedience trial, she sent Maddux to retrieve a dumbbell over a wooden jump. When he landed, he pounced on the dumbbell, started playing with it, and knocked it out of the ring.

The judge picked up the dumbbell and placed it on the table by the entrance to the ring. Although Maddux had officially flunked the class, they went on to the next exercise. Never one to leave a job unfinished, he leaped over the broad jump and ran straight to the table, retrieved his dumbbell, and returned to Dena, executing a perfect *sit*.

working breeds—for example, Rottweilers and Doberman Pinschers. The Group winner then competes for Best in Show against the winners in Herding, Sporting, Non-Sporting, Hounds, Toys, and Terriers. Breed clubs also hold all-Boxer regional and national specialty shows.

If you think you are interested in conformation, have your dog evaluated by some experts. If your Boxer was purchased as a pet, he may have a minor flaw that eliminates him from eligibility, such as being too tall or having a crooked tooth. If your dog isn't show quality, don't be disappointed. These small faults may keep him out of the show ring, but he is eligible to compete in many other dog sports.

If you decide to pursue conformation, join a breed club. Make friends with people who can mentor you as you begin your show career. Take handling classes and learn about competing while you wait to purchase your first show dog.

HERDING

Most people don't think of Boxers as a herding breed, yet they were used for moving cattle on feedlots in the late 19th/early 20th centuries in Germany. Today's Boxers, like some other working breeds—Rottweilers, Samoyeds, and Giant Schnauzers—are returning to their roots and competing in herding events. The American Herding Breed Association (AHBA, www.ahba-herding.org) allows Boxers to earn titles. The AKC is expected to add Boxers to the list of its accepted herding breeds soon. Meanwhile, Boxer lovers are training in anticipation of future AKC acceptance.

In the AHBA, a dog starts by taking a herding instinct test. After passing two tests, he moves on to trials, which are set up like other canine sports. There are three levels and titles in each division. Qualifying scores earn a leg toward a title, and you must qualify in two trials. Dogs compete in Herding Trial Dog competition where they work on a specified course, or Herding Ranch Dog, conducted in a ranch setting. There are also Ranch-Large Flock and Herding Trial Arena Dog divisions. The Herding Trial Championship (HTCh) is awarded to a dog who has earned an advanced title on any one of the trial courses.

The AHBA also offers Junior Herding Tests for dogs who are in training and not yet ready for trials.

OBEDIENCE

AKC obedience competitions showcase your Boxer's ability to work as a team with his handler while performing various obedience cues. In a trial, each team that earns a score of 170 points out of 200 earns a "leg." A title requires earning three legs from at least two different judges.

In the Novice class, your dog earns the Companion Dog (CD) title. You then

Obedience competitions showcase a Boxer's ability to work as a team with his handler while performing various obedience cues.

move up to Open (Companion Dog Excellent, or CDX) and Utility (Utility Dog, or UD). Once you've finished, owners continue competing and earn Utility Dog Excellent (UDX) or the ultimate title, Obedience Trial Champion (OTCH).

The Novice exercises include heeling both on leash and off, *recall*, return to *heel* position ("finish"), stand for examination by the judge, a one-minute *sit*, and a three-minute *down*, all in response to the judge's commands. Some trials offer the Beginner Novice class, where the exercises are easier and conducted completely on leash.

As you move up to Open and Utility classes, the exercises become more challenging, including a *stay* with the handler out of sight, retrieving over a jump, and responding to hand signals from a distance. Dogs are judged on their precision and compliance with the handler's commands.

RALLY OBEDIENCE

Rally is not as structured as regular obedience trials. You move with your dog through a series of stations at your own pace and perform an obedience exercise at each. You can talk to and encourage your dog, and he doesn't have to be in perfect position every second. Although the individual exercises are similar—*heel, sit, down,* about turn, return to *heel* position—judges evaluate teamwork more than precision handling.

There are three levels in AKC rally: Novice, Advanced, and Excellent. You earn a title by getting three qualifying scores of at least 70 out of 100 points from two different judges. The top achievement is the Rally Advanced Excellent (RAE) title.

SCHUTZHUND

The sport of Schutzhund originated in Germany and tests a dog's abilities in tracking, obedience, and protection. A dog must pass all three phases in one trial to earn his Schutzhund title. In the early part of the 20th century, German Boxers were required to have a Schutzhund title before they could be bred.

Today, the Fédération Cynologique Internationale (FCI, www.fci.be), a worldwide canine organization, sets the rules for Schutzhund tests through its IPO arm (International Pruefungsordnung, which means International Trial Rules). Requirements for a title are similar throughout the world. The United States Boxer Association (www.usboxer.org) sponsors events, as do several all-breed Schutzhund clubs like the American Working Dog Federation (AWDF) and United Schutzhund Clubs of America (USA).

Schutzhund rules require the dog to pass a preliminary BH test ("Begleithundprüfung," which means "traffic-sure companion dog"). Next there are three competitive levels—SchH1, SchH2, and SchH3—each more difficult. In addition to SchHI/II/III, dogs may also earn advanced tracking titles: FH1 and FH2; a watchdog title, WH; and an endurance title, AD. In the US, dogs are allowed to compete in obedience and/or tracking and earn titles (OB I/II/III and TR I/II/III) without competing in the protection phase.

Any owner who wants to compete in protection must first compete in tracking and obedience. There are no separate protection titles like there are for obedience and tracking. In protection work, the dog finds an assistant or "decoy" who is hiding and prevents him from escaping by biting his heavily padded sleeve, which the decoy wears specifically for the test. The dog must release the decoy on command, showing that he is under control even in an excited state.

In a tracking test, the dog follows a human scent and recovers a glove at the end of the track while the handler follows.

TRACKING

If you are not interested in the intensity of Schutzhund training, you can still teach your Boxer to track and earn titles. Join a tracking club or class and train with other people who can lay tracks for you and teach you how to "read" your dog's actions.

In an AKC tracking test, the dog follows a human scent and recovers a glove at the end of the track while the handler follows. Unlike other dog sports, which require a dog to qualify three times, you only need to complete one track successfully to earn a title. At the beginning level, the dog follows a 440- to 500-yard (402.5- to 457-m) track that includes several changes of direction. If successful, he earns his Tracking Dog (TD) title. To complete the next level (Tracking Dog Excellent, or TDX), he must follow a track that is older, longer, and more difficult. Variable Surface Tracking (VST) tests a dog's ability to track in an urban setting over concrete, asphalt, and other less natural surfaces. A dog who completes all three titles earns the Champion Tracker (CT) title.

NONCOMPETITIVE ACTIVITIES

If you're not excited about performance or competitive sports, there are plenty of other fun and relaxing ways you and your Boxer can enjoy time together.

BOXER GET-TOGETHERS

Your community may have groups of Boxer fans that meet weekly or monthly. Owners convene at parks, trails, beaches, and homes to share their love for Boxers and have fun with their dogs. For example, an Internet search for Boxers on www.meetup.com turned up more than 262 members in the Seattle area. If there isn't a group in your area, you can start one.

BOXER RESCUE

Thousands of Boxers end up homeless each year, either as strays or shelter dogs. If you don't have room in your home for another pet, you can still give back to the breed by volunteering for Boxer rescue. Volunteers check shelters, transport dogs, provide foster homes, work at adoption fairs, and provide other support. You'll make friends with other Boxer owners and be able to bring your dog to social events, parades, and public outreach events.

CANINE GOOD CITIZEN® PROGRAM

Boxers, with their cropped ears and muscular frames, present an imposing image to people not familiar with the breed. In addition, they are sometimes confused with breeds that have a reputation for aggressiveness. A well-behaved Boxer serves as a goodwill ambassador for the breed.

Available to all dogs whether or not they have registration papers, the AKC Canine Good Citizen (CGC) program honors well-behaved dogs and responsible dog owners. A dog must complete the following ten exercises; if successful, he earns a CGC certificate:

1. accept a stranger stopping to talk with you
2. sit still and accept petting by a stranger
3. allow someone to handle him as a groomer or veterinarian would

A well-behaved Boxer serves as a goodwill ambassador for the breed.

4. walk nicely on a loose leash
5. walk nicely through a crowd
6. sit and lie down on command and stay in position as you walk away
7. come when called
8. remain calm in the presence of another dog
9. react confidently to distractions
10. accept being left alone with someone else without becoming overly anxious

Dog clubs, trainers, and therapy dog evaluators often host CGC classes and tests. Find a list of evaluators in your area on the AKC's website: www.akc.org/events/cgc/cgc_bystate.cfm.

DOG PARKS

Although not all Boxers are social with other dogs, if yours is, dog parks are a good place to help him burn off all that excess Boxer enthusiasm. For everyone's safety, choose a park that separates large dogs from small ones.

A park is only as good as the owners who visit it. It is the owner's responsibility to keep an eye on the dog and stop rough play before it gets out of hand. If there are aggressive dogs or inattentive owners, leave. Responsible dog park visitors also clean up after their dogs.

THERAPY WORK

Boxers are so intuitive and adept at reading a person's emotions that they make exceptional therapy dogs. Therapy dogs visit schools, nursing homes, hospitals, and libraries. Many dog trainers offer classes where you and your dog learn the necessary skills. Therapy Dogs International (www.tdi-dog.org) and the Delta Society (www.deltasociety.org) are national organizations with local chapters that train and certify therapy dogs. The Delta Society also provides a home study course to prepare you for visits. In addition to purely social visits, you and your dog can undergo advanced training to assist doctors and therapists with actual therapy and rehabilitation sessions.

Most organizations require that a therapy dog pass the Canine Good Citizen test. They then conduct an additional evaluation to observe how he deals with the various sights, sounds, and smells he will encounter. For example, your Boxer must react calmly around wheelchairs, walkers, and loud noises.

ACTIVITIES FOR CHILDREN

Boxers love kids, and there are several activities in which children can learn about dogs and enjoy time with their pets:

4-H

4-H (which stands for "head, heart, hands, and health") was originally an agricultural organization operating mostly in rural communities. Today, 4-H groups are active in all 50 states. They are operated by your state extension service, offering children ages 5 to 19 hands-on learning programs that help them develop life skills. This includes clubs that give kids the opportunity to train and show their dogs. Many exhibit their dogs at county and state fairs. Children enter classes such as "fitting and showing," where the dog is judged based on the grooming and care he has received. The handler is judged on attitude, appearance, knowledge, and ability to handle the dog. Learn more at www.4-H.org.

AKC JUNIOR SHOWMANSHIP

For children who think they want to show dogs in conformation, perhaps even professionally, the AKC developed the Junior Showmanship program (www.akc. org/kids_juniors/jr_getting_started.cfm). Children aged 9 to 18 get a chance to learn about dogs and dog shows, sharpen their handling skills, and practice good sportsmanship.

You don't need a show-quality Boxer to enter Junior Showmanship, although your dog must be registered and eligible to enter shows in either conformation or obedience.

Juniors are judged on their ability to present their dogs the same way that dogs are shown in the breed ring, except the focus is on the handler. The quality of the junior's presentation, not the quality of the dog, is judged. Juniors are encouraged to develop their handling abilities, dress appropriately, conduct themselves in a proper manner, and keep the dog in well-groomed condition.

Even if they don't pursue the sport professionally, showing dogs is a hobby that many children go on to enjoy throughout their lives.

With some preparation, your Boxer can accompany the family on vacations.

BOY/GIRL SCOUTS

For dog-loving children, both the Boy and Girl Scouts offer pet care merit badges. Children demonstrate that they have cared for a dog, researched care and health, and learned about responsible pet ownership. Boy Scouts can earn the Dog Care Merit Badge (www.boyscouttrail.com/boy-scouts/meritbadges/dogcare.asp), Junior Girl Scouts (www.girlscouts.org) can earn the Pet Care badge, and Brownies participate in the Animal Care "Try-It."

TRAVELING WITH YOUR BOXER

With some preparation, your Boxer can accompany the family on vacations. Here are some tips to help you plan for his trip:

- **Cleanup supplies:** Pack cleanup bags, pooper-scooper, and an odor neutralizer. Responsible dog owners clean up after their pets in highway rest areas and parks as well as hotel doggy areas. If pet owners don't pick up after their pets, more and more facilities won't allow dogs in the future. Dogs also might carry seeds of non-native plants in their feces, and the resulting growth disrupts native habitats.
- **Crate train:** If he is not already crate trained, now is the time to teach him to spend time confined. He'll be safer in a hotel room, an unfamiliar home, in the car, or on a plane if he is already comfortable spending time in his crate.
- **Food:** Bring enough of his regular food so that you won't run out. Traveling is stressful, and you don't want to add more upset by suddenly changing his diet.
- **Health certificate:** If you are crossing state lines you are required to carry a health certificate issued by a veterinarian, usually within the last 30 days. It confirms the dog's rabies vaccine and other health information. Requirements vary by state.
- **Heartworm preventive:** If your dog is not already on a heartworm preventive, have him tested and start him on a monthly medication. There are very few states where heartworm is not a problem, so protect your Boxer before you leave home.
- **Hotels/parks:** As you plan your itinerary, check with family members, hotels, and campgrounds to be sure that your Boxer is welcome. For example, although dogs are allowed in national parks, they aren't allowed on every trail or in every campground.

- **ID tag/microchip:**
  Update his tags with
  your cell phone number
  so that you can be
  reached when you are
  away from home. Carry
  his microchip info and
  the registry's phone
  number with you. If
  he is lost, contact the
  registry immediately.

- **Toys and bed:** Bring his bed, toys, or blanket to make unfamiliar surroundings smell like home.

TRAVEL BY CAR

The following tips will help you travel by car with your Boxer more safely and easily:

- Crate your dog while you are driving. You don't need a rowdy canine bouncing around while you're negotiating mountain roads. If you're in an accident, your dog could be thrown against the dashboard or windows and badly injured. He could be also thrown from the car and run off, terrified.
- You've heard the motto "Buckle up for safety." That goes for dogs as well as kids. If you can't crate your dog, purchase a canine seat belt or make a restraint from a walking harness. Both dogs and kids settle down faster if everyone is strapped in.
- Heat is especially dangerous to Boxers. Be sure that your dog gets fresh air and is shielded from direct sun. And never leave him alone in a car; he could overheat and die in minutes.
- Carry your own water from home if at all possible to prevent tummy upset. Stop every two or three hours for a drink and a potty break. Dehydration is just as dangerous as overheating.
- Get medication for carsickness from your vet before you leave. Winding roads can quickly upset even the healthiest dog's tummy.
- Leash your dog when you and your dog are not in the car. A sudden noise or the sight of a squirrel might cause him to run away. Rest areas and unfamiliar neighborhoods are not the places to test his training. Also, an off-leash dog will often run up to strangers and frighten them.

BOXER

TRAVEL BY AIR

Many airlines refuse to transport brachycephalic breeds like Boxers, Pugs, and Bulldogs because their facial structure makes them so susceptible to heat exhaustion. Check with the airline when you make your reservations, because regulations vary. If you do decide to fly your Boxer, try to schedule a nonstop flight. Don't take a chance that workers might leave your dog on the hot tarmac or in a cargo hold between flights. In the summer, travel at night when temperatures are cooler. Many airlines won't fly animals at temperatures under 35°F (1.5°C) or over 85°F (29.5°C).

Airlines require solid plastic crates that are big enough for your dog to stand up and turn around in. You must also supply a water bowl (clip-on style) and some food. Write your contact information and the dog's name on the crate so that airline staff sees it.

The American Veterinary Medical Association (AVMA) does not recommend tranquilizing dogs for flying. Specifically, avoid using the tranquilizer acepromazine because Boxers are known to have an adverse, possibly fatal, reaction to it. Sedatives can cause respiratory problems when combined with pressure from high altitude, even in a dog with normal facial structure. Discuss this option with your veterinarian if you think that a tranquilizer is necessary. Note the name of the drug, dosage, and time administered on the crate so that airline personnel are aware of it.

Many vacation destinations can be Boxer-friendly.

PET-FRIENDLY LODGING

Many hotels, campgrounds, and RV parks welcome dogs as their guests. Check ahead to find out specific rules and regulations and whether there are any specific breed or size restrictions. You'll find that some hotels offer special amenities for your Boxer, like dog day care, off-leash play areas, special bowls, and treats. Hotels usually charge an extra nightly fee for each pet.

Most facilities have a limited number of pet-friendly rooms, so book your reservations in advance. As they limit rooms for smokers, they must also keep some allergen-free.

RESOURCES

ASSOCIATIONS AND ORGANIZATIONS

BREED CLUBS

American Boxer Club (ABC)
www.americanboxerclub.org

American Kennel Club (AKC)
5580 Centerview Drive
Raleigh, NC 27606
Telephone: (919) 233-9767
Fax: (919) 233-3627
E-Mail: info@akc.org
www.akc.org

British Boxer Club
www.thebritishboxerclub.co.uk

Canadian Kennel Club (CKC)
89 Skyway Avenue, Suite 100
Etobicoke, Ontario M9W 6R4
Telephone: (416) 675-5511
Fax: (416) 675-6506
E-Mail: information@ckc.ca
www.ckc.ca

Federation Cynologique Internationale (FCI)
Secretariat General de la FCI
Place Albert 1er, 13
B – 6530 Thuin
Belqique
www.fci.be

The Kennel Club
1 Clarges Street
London
W1J 8AB
Telephone: 0870 606 6750
Fax: 0207 518 1058
www.the-kennel-club.org.uk

United Kennel Club (UKC)
100 E. Kilgore Road
Kalamazoo, MI 49002-5584
Telephone: (269) 343-9020
Fax: (269) 343-7037
E-Mail: pbickell@ukcdogs.com
www.ukcdogs.com

PET SITTERS

National Association of Professional Pet Sitters
15000 Commerce Parkway, Suite C
Mt. Laurel, New Jersey 08054
Telephone: (856) 439-0324
Fax: (856) 439-0525
E-Mail: napps@ahint.com
www.petsitters.org

Pet Sitters International
201 East King Street
King, NC 27021-9161
Telephone: (336) 983-9222
Fax: (336) 983-5266
E-Mail: info@petsit.com
www.petsit.com

RESCUE ORGANIZATIONS AND ANIMAL WELFARE GROUPS

American Humane Association (AHA)
63 Inverness Drive East
Englewood, CO 80112
Telephone: (303) 792-9900
Fax: 792-5333
www.americanhumane.org

American Society for the Prevention of Cruelty to Animals (ASPCA)
424 E. 92nd Street
New York, NY 10128-6804
Telephone: (212) 876-7700
www.aspca.org

The Humane Society of the United States (HSUS)
2100 L Street, NW
Washington DC 20037
Telephone: (202) 452-1100
www.hsus.org

Royal Society for the Prevention of Cruelty to Animals (RSPCA)
RSPCA Enquiries Service
Wilberforce Way, Southwater,
Horsham, West Sussex RH13 9RS
United Kingdom
Telephone: 0870 3335 999
Fax: 0870 7530 284
www.rspca.org.uk

SPORTS

International Agility Link (IAL)
Global Administrator: Steve Drinkwater
E-Mail: yunde@powerup.au
www.agilityclick.com/~ial

The World Canine Freestyle Organization, Inc.
P.O. Box 350122
Brooklyn, NY 11235
Telephone: (718) 332-8336
Fax: (718) 646-2686
E-Mail: WCFODOGS@aol.com
www.worldcaninefreestyle.org

THERAPY

Delta Society
875 124th Ave, NE, Suite 101
Bellevue, WA 98005
Telephone: (425) 679-5500
Fax: (425) 679-5539
E-Mail: info@DeltaSociety.org
www.deltasociety.org

Therapy Dogs Inc.
P.O. Box 20227
Cheyenne WY 82003
Telephone: (877) 843-7364
Fax: (307) 638-2079
E-Mail: therapydogsinc@
qwestoffice.net
www.therapydogs.com

Therapy Dogs International (TDI)
88 Bartley Road
Flanders, NJ 07836
Telephone: (973) 252-9800
Fax: (973) 252-7171
E-Mail: tdi@gti.net
www.tdi-dog.org

TRAINING

Association of Pet Dog Trainers (APDT)
101 North Main St, Suite 610
Greenville, SC 29615
Telephone: (800) PET-DOGS
Fax: (864) 331-0767
E-Mail: information@apdt.com
www.apdt.com

International Association of Animal Behavior Consultants (IAABC)
565 Callery Road
Cranberry Township, PA 16066
E-Mail: info@iaabc.org
www.iaabc.org

National Association of Dog Obedience Instructors (NADOI)
PMB 369
729 Grapevine Hwy.
Hurst, TX 76054-2085
www.nadoi.org

VETERINARY AND HEALTH RESOURCES

Academy of Veterinary Homeopathy (AVH)
P.O. Box 9280
Wilmington, DE 19809
Telephone: (866) 652-1590
Fax: (866) 652-1590
www.theavh.org

American Academy of Veterinary Acupuncture (AAVA)
P.O. Box 1058
Glastonbury, CT 06033
Telephone: (860) 632-9911
Fax: (860) 659-8772
www.aava.org

American Animal Hospital Association (AAHA)
12575 W. Bayaud Ave.
Lakewood, CO 80228
Telephone: (303) 986-2800
Fax: (303) 986-1700
E-Mail: info@aahanet.org
www.aahanet.org/index.cfm

American College of Veterinary Internal Medicine (ACVIM)
1997 Wadsworth Blvd., Suite A
Lakewood, CO 80214-5293
Telephone: (800) 245-9081
Fax: (303) 231-0880
Email: ACVIM@ACVIM.org
www.acvim.org

American College of Veterinary Ophthalmologists (ACVO)
P.O. Box 1311
Meridian, ID 83860
Telephone: (208) 466-7624
Fax: (208) 466-7693
E-Mail: office09@acvo.com
www.acvo.com

American Holistic Veterinary Medical Association (AHVMA)
2218 Old Emmorton Road
Bel Air, MD 21015
Telephone: (410) 569-0795
Fax: (410) 569-2346
E-Mail: office@ahvma.org
www.ahvma.org

American Veterinary Medical Association (AVMA)
1931 North Meacham Road, Suite 100
Schaumburg, IL 60173-4360
Telephone: (847) 925-8070
Fax: (847) 925-1329
E-Mail: avmainfo@avma.org
www.avma.org

ASPCA Animal Poison Control Center
Telephone: (888) 426-4435
www.aspca.org

British Veterinary Association (BVA)
7 Mansfield Street
London
W1G 9NQ
Telephone: 0207 636 6541
Fax: 0207 908 6349
E-Mail: bvahq@bva.co.uk
www.bva.co.uk

Canine Eye Registration Foundation (CERF)
VMDB/CERF
1717 Philo Rd
P O Box 3007
Urbana, IL 61803-3007
Telephone: (217) 693-4800
Fax: (217) 693-4801
E-Mail: CERF@vmbd.org
www.vmdb.org

Orthopedic Foundation for Animals (OFA)
2300 NE Nifong Blvd
Columbus, Missouri 65201-3856
Telephone: (573) 442-0418
Fax: (573) 875-5073
Email: ofa@offa.org
www.offa.org

US Food and Drug Administration Center for Veterinary Medicine (CVM)
7519 Standish Place
HFV-12
Rockville, MD 20855-0001
Telephone: (240) 276-9300 or (888) INFO-FDA
http://www.fda.gov/cvm

PUBLICATIONS
BOOKS

Anderson, Teoti. *The Super Simple Guide to Housetraining.* Neptune City: TFH Publications, 2004.

Anne, Jonna, with Mary Straus. *The Healthy Dog Cookbook: 50 Nutritious and Delicious Recipes Your Dog Will Love.* UK: Ivy Press Limited, 2008.

Boneham, Sheila Webster, Ph.D. Terra-Nova *The Boxer.* Neptune City: TFH Publications, Inc., 2005.

Dainty, Suellen. *50 Games to Play With Your Dog.* UK: Ivy Press Limited, 2007.

Gallagher, Cynthia P. DogLife *Boxer.* Neptune City: TFH Publications, Inc., 2010.

—. Animal Planet *Boxers.* Neptune City: TFH Publications, Inc., 2006.

MAGAZINES
AKC Family Dog
American Kennel Club
260 Madison Avenue
New York, NY 10016
Telephone: (800) 490-5675
E-Mail: familydog@akc.org
www.akc.org/pubs/familydog

AKC Gazette
American Kennel Club
260 Madison Avenue
New York, NY 10016
Telephone: (800) 533-7323
E-Mail: gazette@akc.org
www.akc.org/pubs/gazette

Dog & Kennel
Pet Publishing, Inc.
7-L Dundas Circle
Greensboro, NC 27407
Telephone: (336) 292-4272
Fax: (336) 292-4272
E-Mail: info@petpublishing.com
www.dogandkennel.com

Dogs Monthly
Ascot House
High Street, Ascot,
Berkshire SL5 7JG
United Kingdom
Telephone: 0870 730 8433
Fax: 0870 730 8431
E-Mail: admin@rtc-associates.freeserve.co.uk
www.corsini.co.uk/dogsmonthly

WEBSITES
Nylabone
www.nylabone.com

TFH Publications, Inc.
www.tfh.com

INDEX

Note: **Boldfaced** numbers indicate illustrations.

PHOTO CREDITS

Terry Albert: 24, 28

Bull's-Eye Arts (Shutterstock.com): 13

Alexander Bark (Shutterstock.com): 106

Joy Brown (Shutterstock.com): 29, 62, 76

R Carner (Shutterstock.com): 64

Diego Cervo (Shutterstock.com): 66

James Clarke (Shutterstock.com): 125

cynoclub (Shutterstock.com): 15, 77, 116

Melanie DeFazio (Shutterstock.com): 120

Tad Denson (Shutterstock.com): 83, 97

FotoJagodka (Shutterstock.com): 101

Gayvoronskaya_yana (Shutterstock.com): 53

Karen Givens (Shutterstock.com): 61

Guilu (Shutterstock.com): 54

Tracy Hendrickson: 4, 7, 11, 16, 68, 69, 70, 73, 86, 90, 96, 99, 108, 118, 124, 127, 133

Damian Herde (Shutterstock.com): 85

Anna Hoychuk (Shutterstock.com): 58, 113

terekhov igor (Shutterstock.com): 38

Eric Isselée (Shutterstock.com): 1, 3

Rolf Klebsattel (Shutterstock.com): 129

George Lee (Shutterstock.com): 42, 112, 122

Donald Linscott (Shutterstock.com): 100

Victoria Veluz and Alexandra Lozano: 30, 32, 36, 40, 46, 49

Adam Majchrzak (Shutterstock.com): 81

mathom (Shutterstock.com): 57

mjt (Shutterstock.com): 20

david woodberry Pure Eye Photo (Shutterstock.com): 18

South 12th Photography (Shutterstock.com): 26

Dramatic Paws Animal Photography (Shutterstock.com): 88

Morgan Lane Photography (Shutterstock.com): 105

inacio pires (Shutterstock.com): 22

Gastev Roman (Shutterstock.com): 6

Susan Schmitz (Shutterstock.com): front cover, back cover

Pavel Semenov (Shutterstock.com): 48

Jana Shea (Shutterstock.com): 80

Shutterstock (Shutterstock.com): 44, 52, 92

Stana (Shutterstock.com): 79

Zoran Tripalo (Shutterstock.com): 21

upthebanner (Shutterstock.com): 74

Vukoslavovic (Shutterstock.com): 33

Whytock (Shutterstock.com): 110

All other photos courtesy of Isabelle Francais and TFH archives.

DEDICATION

This book is dedicated to my loyal friends who have supported and encouraged me through my winding career path.

ACKNOWLEDGMENTS

Thank you to the many friends and Boxer experts who helped me with my research. Among them: Cindy Jobs, Lois and George Trist, Bridget Reinhold, Tracy Hendrickson, Mark Chase, Sarbit Singh, DVM, Liz Palika, Dena Hudson, Dale Rigtrup, Terry Parrish, Annette Hake, Peggy Weiss, AN Sunder, Karon Adams, and Suzie Campbell.

ABOUT THE AUTHOR

Award-winning writer and artist **Terry Albert** has been working with dogs for more than 25 years. Her experience with dogs, cats, horses, animal rescue, dog training, and pet sitting has given her up-close experience with many breeds,

including Boxers. She has previously written books about Basset Hounds and Labrador Retrievers. Her writing credits include Petco, PetDoc.com, Delta Society, and numerous websites and newsletters. She has won several Maxwell Awards from the Dog Writers Association of America (DWAA) for her artwork and writing and served as the DWAA annual writing competition chair in 2005, 2006, and 2009.

Terry has served on the Board of Directors for Seattle Purebred Dog Rescue, LabMed, and the Humane Society of Seattle/King Co. Terry is also a past recipient of the Channel 10 San Diego Leadership Award for her volunteer work. She has boarded dogs in her home for more than ten years and currently has several Boxers who are regular houseguests.

Terry works out of her home in Poway, California, where she lives with her four dogs, three horses, two cats, and two box turtles.

ABOUT ANIMAL PLANET™

Animal Planet™ is the only television network dedicated exclusively to the connection between humans and animals. The network brings people of all ages together by tapping into our fundamental fascination with animals through an array of fresh programming that includes humor, competition, drama, and spectacle from the animal kingdom.

ABOUT *DOGS 101*

The most comprehensive—and most endearing—dog encyclopedia on television, *DOGS 101* spotlights the adorable, the feisty and the unexpected. A wide-ranging rundown of everyone's favorite dog breeds—from the Dalmatian to Xoloitzcuintli —this series surveys a variety of breeds for their behavioral quirks, genetic history, most famous examples and wildest trivia. Learn which dogs are best for urban living and which would be the best fit for your family. Using a mix of animal experts, pop-culture footage and stylized dog photography, *DOGS 101* is an unprecedented look at man's best friend.